THE CHURCH ON THE MOVE

DIVISION OF THE SOCIETY OF ST. PAUL

alba house
STATEN ISLAND, N.Y. 10314

THE CHURCH
ON THE MOVE

Bernard Häring, C.Ss.R.

First published under the title: *Zusage an die Welt* by Verlag
Gerhard Kaffke, Bergen-Enkheim bei Frankfurt/Main.

Library of Congress Catalog Card Number: 72-129175

SBN: 8189-0192-6

Contents

Introduction

The individual chapters of this book examine from various angles the question of a Christian world concept and of the responsibility of Christians for the actual condition of the world today.

Not only in other religions but in Christianity too there have occasionally emerged conceptions of spiritual salvation and morality which estranged man from the world and from life itself. The Christian of today speaks less of "salvation" than of the sanctification of the whole person through the believer's response to God's saving love and a true concept of God and of ourselves.

But it sometimes happens that a person, although fundamentally willing to accept the concept of God, is nevertheless in some way a fugitive from the hard world of economic, social and political values. Such a man abandons the unregenerate world to its government, institutions, and public opinion, unless he urgently needs it for his own purposes. But here we are concerned with trying to understand the individual's attitude to the world which is evolved from a clear perception of the world forces all around him; we are concerned with a passionate love of the world through which the human being finds himself and God and other people. If he despises the world, he fails to find himself or to develop his best qualities.

We are dealing with a personal approach which must take into consideration the variety of individuals' wave-lengths before an attempt can be made to reform the world in the service of mankind. When he praises the Lord, the Christian is not being "unworldly," for it is in the worship of God, "in spirit and in truth," that he experiences most profoundly the truth that religion is life and involves an apostolate to the world. In order to promote an understanding of the world, according to the aims of the Second Vatican Council and of modern theologians, it is absolutely necessary to abolish the gulf between religion and life.

The mature Christian realizes that the genuineness of all religious belief is proved by its fruits. The union of faith, hope and love is light for the world, offering a loving alternative to the world's belief in brotherhood, social justice and peace. Whoever believes in the Savior of the world will, both as an individual and as a member of society, make good use of his freedom in order to "humanize" the world.

Faith in the Lord of history means a willing acceptance of today's reality. An ethical code based on religion necessarily presents the question: How can an ethical code whose rules were established by revelation in former times be acceptable to the men and the world of today? The Sermon on the Mount seems to me to offer the key to the solution of this question.

The sublimity of the demands it makes on us is the proof of God's merciful love for mankind and for his world. God is always with the world and speaks through it. In faith, and in the knowledge of God and Christ, the living human being becomes increasingly aware of the actual world around him. Our Omega, the love of Christ, gives us final freedom in our constant effort to devote ourselves to the service of mankind. We do not say that in this way the tensions in the world are all resolved, but that even in the midst of these we are offered salvation and the love of Christ.

Chapter I

The Church on the Move: Man and the World

The Pastoral Constitution of the Second Vatican Council, "The Church in the Modern World" (*Gaudium et Spes*)[1] reflects, perhaps more than any other Conciliar document, the characteristic spirit of the Council. It was the last Council text to be commissioned and came as a sort of conclusion to all the others. Therefore it was the one which could most successfully sum up everything that was particularly characteristic of this Council. Here it was a question of breaking new ground, for no Council had ever yet set itself a similar task. Only in retrospect, when the epoch ushered in by the Second Vatican Council has borne its fruits, can we hope to be able to form a mature and comprehensive judgment of all the new ways of thought it suggests and, more especially, of all the new prospects which it has opened up. Some of these have already been courageously explored, while others are only timidly indicated or even quietly ignored. From the abundant material provided for our consideration we shall, in the following notes, only deal with whatever, in our opinion, may be regarded as particularly significant for the future.

THE TITLE: PASTORAL CONSTITUTION

To many Council Fathers of the old school

it seemed a contradiction in terms to put together the two words "Constitution" and "Pastoral" in order to form a single organic entity. For them "Constitution" meant simply doctrine, whereas "Pastoral" meant practical applications of the doctrine. But it is precisely this title, which indicates a synthesis, and the content which corresponds to this synthesis, that shows us what is understood by the description of the Second Vatican Council as a "Pastoral Council."

The first paragraph of the footnote is particularly decisive: "The Constitution is called 'Pastoral' because, although based on doctrinal principles, it seeks to express the attitude of the Church to the world and modern man. The result is that as pastoral considerations are not missing from the first part, so doctrinal considerations are not missing from the second." Then an indication is given of the task awaiting theologians: they are not to confuse the permanent content of doctrine with the historical environmental material which has helped to determine its presentation and a whole series of its directives. Most valuable also is the explicit assertion that theologians must reckon with the fact that some parts of the document deal with questions which by their very nature reflect changes due to historical evolution.

As the outlook for the theology of the post-Conciliar epoch becomes clearer, we see a more determined attitude, especially in the conclusions reached in the *Constitution on Divine Revelation*: Theology must regard all historical documents, including the Bible, as a revelation of truth and salvation given at a definite moment in history. For its full understanding, one cannot disregard the actual circumstances of that historical moment, of the men who received this revelation and of their particular requirements. The sociological application of science and of the history of culture is increasingly recognized as a necessary auxiliary to theology. The pronouncements of the past centuries must be stripped by theologians of their original environmental material and placed in the environment of the present day, with great respect for their permanent content and a loving understanding of the people of our own time with their own particular sensibilities, their readiness to listen and their ability to hear.

STARTING POINT: SIGNS OF THE TIMES

In order to avoid any misunderstandings, let it be said that the final and most authentic starting point for the Church is always Christ and the truth of salvation which he revealed.

4

We are speaking here of the starting point of the dialogue with the world. The logical use of the inductive method necessitates first of all the questions: How must we define the partners in this dialogue? What are the facts about the situation in which the Church and world find themselves? What significance do we attribute — each in his own way — to the events and circumstances of the present day?

In the *Pastoral Constitution on the Church in the Modern World* we find the successful application of an idea dominant in the mind of Pope John XXIII. Here we see a kind of pastoral sociology deliberately devoting itself to the cause of salvation and working in the light of faith. It has already proved its validity and fruitfulness in the service of the Church. Here is something which the best theologians have always presented in a less self-conscious way, but which is now presented in full consciousness of its import and raised to the status of a method.

It reflects the eternal topicality of the message of salvation, and the participation of the Church in the life of every epoch. But this is not all. The very expression "signs of the times," from which a very prolonged and laborious sub-commission for Schema 13 took

its name, indicates a profound truth rooted in the faith. God has undoubtedly given us his final and authentic message in Christ. The revelation of the Word, in its strictest sense, ends with the era of the apostles. But since all events are ordained by the Word of God, in which all things were created and are finally directed to Christ, history itself is in its own way a theological manifestation. In the material of history which naturally contains also his revelation in Christ, God continues to declare to us his purposes.

Her humble, alert and responsive attitude to the signs of the times reveals the true character of the Church, so unlike the synagogue in the times of Jesus which misread the signs of the times because it was estranged from life and imprisoned in a punctilious literal interpretation of the written word. Although Christianity possesses the noblest of all books, it is not essentially a "book religion." The Bible provides us with an authentic record of the substance and meaning of God's dealings with his people and of their response to him. It must be read and interpreted in relation to the whole historical process of salvation, of which we are a part.

A respectable minority, which included many fervent admirers of Pope John, was for a time

The joys and hopes, the griefs and the
anxieties of the men of this age, especially
those who are poor or in any way afflicted,
these too are the joys and hopes,
the griefs and anxieties of the
followers of Christ.   no. 1

very sceptical in its attitude because it was thought that this Constitution was, in practice, little more than a "peg-board" on which everything (trousers, coats, skirts and aprons) for which there was no room elsewhere, was to be hung. But this anxiety was not entirely justified. In spite of the variety of the individual problems it deals with, the Constitution has a spiritual unity which became clearly apparent only when the Schema was adopted by a central sub-commission. One of the most decisive influences for the promotion of unity is indeed an awareness of the "signs of the times" and a thoughtful understanding of the man of today in relation to the story of salvation.

In order to show how decisive this new attitude was one need only compare the section about "Marriage and the Family," drawn up by the preparatory theological Commission, with the corresponding chapter in the second part of the Pastoral Constitution *Gaudium et Spes* (The Church in the Modern World) as it reads today. The former sketch was as complete as possible a collection of the pronouncements of all epochs, almost like an historical survey of an unhistorical point of view. In contrast to this, the text finally approved of by the Council Fathers was inspired not only by the authority of the Bible but also by a study of the actual conditions of marriage and married people today. Even if it cannot provide a ready answer to all the questions now put forward with such urgency, it is nevertheless a great step forward that these problems should at last have been keenly examined and recognized as requiring an answer.

The question of methods of birth control, for example, which in *Casti Connubii* was given central prominence and treated from a non-historical point of view, being largely formulated and answered from the standpoint of a fast disappearing epoch, has now, without being thereby in any way minimized, been moved into a wider sphere, that of responsible parenthood and the deliberate cultivation of conjugal love, based on absolute fidelity and exposed to many different kinds of danger. The concept of love now takes the central place — a love redeemed, at once sanctified and sanctifying, and demanding mutual loyalty. It gives happiness but demands self-denial and generous, fruitful mutual self-giving. In this way it expresses the noblest longings of our epoch but, like the Bible, sets itself against many legalistic neo-Platonic and Stoic elements superimposed in former times.

THE ART OF DIALOGUE: A SEARCH FOR COMMON ELEMENTS

The Constitution *Gaudium et Spes* shows very visibly the characteristic imprint of the Pope who summoned the Council, John XXIII, namely the principle that one must seek first those elements which unite men rather than those which separate them. Even in the Introduction we see expressed this basic principle of the unity of all men in their shared joys and hopes, griefs and fears.

As its central theme the Constitution considers all that concerns the extraordinarily broad sphere of interests which the children of the Church share with other men: their existence and activity in this world, their efforts to construct an earthly home and their longing for true brotherhood. They share their economic, social and cultural activities and their response to the basic requirements of existence, such as marriage and the family, the State and the community of nations. These original earthly interests which we have in common nevertheless lead us on to that which is not yet sought and acknowledged by all as a common element, but which is nevertheless in the truest sense a common inheritance: Christ, salvation by faith in him and mutual love for his sake — and all this not as something apart from the life experienced in common but as part and parcel of the stuff of this world.

Dialogue is based on reciprocity, questions and answers from each side. This point of view frequently prevails in *Gaudium et Spes*. One has only to think of the chapter heading: "The Help Which the Church Receives from the Modern World." [2] One is always willing to accept a service from anyone who is himself capable of gratitude, but if a man offers his service in a condescending manner and purely for his own self-satisfaction, then the recipient feels humiliated. But it is not only a case of a psychological reaction, however important this may be in itself. It is also a matter of theological principle: the Church is not a monopolistic society and does not claim to monopolize in herself and for herself the gifts and works of God. She, who has been so uniquely endowed with God's graces, must gratefully honor and acknowledge all that God brings to pass in history, according to his will and for the real good of men.

The spirit of the Council is clearly expressed when it deals with those Christians who are separated from Rome (in the *Decree on Ecumenism*), with other religions (in the *Declaration on the Relationship of the Church to*

Non-Christian Religions) and when it speaks of all the good to be found in the world in *Gaudium et Spes.*

Reciprocity is so extensive that the Church is even able to learn some spiritual truths from her calumniators and persecutors. This is not only explicitly admitted in the above-mentioned paragraph 44, but is also a clearly visible spiritual attitude in paragraphs 19-21 which are concerned with atheism and the Church's attitude to this most alarming phenomenon. Faced with the various forms of atheism today, Christians probe their consciences to try to discover what, in their own conduct, language and worship can have made belief so difficult for so many people. The Church tries to understand the mysterious and frequently distorted aims and desires of atheists in order to examine and present her own authentic message more effectively. While the Church thus learns to listen and to observe she is all the time preparing herself to deliver the message of salvation in a more comprehensible manner.

Against the background of elements shared in common there naturally emerges ever more clearly that element which distinguishes the Church which Christ sent to preach to all men, and that mark which the Lord impressed upon her to set her apart from the world: her message of salvation.

THE MESSAGE: THE SALVATION OF MAN

The Pastoral Constitution has as the object of its consideration the earthly welfare and activity of all men and especially of all Christians; it presents a pastoral view or theology of the world but its aim is always the salvation of men. The Church has no particular competence to judge earthly things and temporal activities, their stark actuality or worldly effectiveness. Her message concerns salvation but the salvation of the whole living being. Therefore she must interpret all human activities and situations in the light of a man's salvation, his *vocatio integra*. She presents her doctrine in such a way as to prepare the whole human person for salvation.

Here the Church must be guided by two main considerations:

1. She must free herself from all traces of the theocratic thought of past ages, making it clear that she does not assert her own sovereignty in every sphere of life, but God's supremacy as Savior and judge. She insists upon a certain rightful independence from ecclesiastical jurisdiction in mundane spheres like those of science, art, culture, economics and politics.

2. The Church restores life to religion, a life

which had often been denied to it because it seemed as if religion intended to leave no room for the development of the life of the individual. The living man, the living Christian who has to learn to distinguish his role as a citizen of this world from his role as a representative of the Church, knows that in all his vital integrity he is dedicated to God. He cannot seek his salvation in God if he remains bound to the earthly realms of unregeneracy and inhumanity.

The Constitution *Gaudium et Spes* is concerned with the salvation of individual men and of all mankind, the salvation which has its sacrament in the Church and which also sheds its light over the whole order of things on earth. The Council expresses the theology of a world which was created by God as part of his great plan of salvation, for it too is his own creation and shares man's thirst for redemption. After being truly redeemed in Christ it longs to share fully in the freedom of God's children. In this way the Constitution repeatedly emphasizes that man's salvation by far transcends the purely spiritual sphere, and that when man seeks salvation in faith he is not thereby estranged from his duties in this world but, on the contrary, is enabled, and indeed bound, to take into serious consideration all earthly obligations and duties.

SCHEMA 13: IN THE LIGHT OF THE GOSPEL

One of the difficult questions which cropped up during the preparations of Schema 13 concerned the plane upon which the Church can begin her dialogue with all men. It seemed to many that it was against the rules of human dialogue for the Church to argue on the plane of revealed faith, since this is not shared by all men. According to these critics the right procedure would have been to gather records from the wealth of human experience of 2,000 years, to assume the cloak of the philosopher and to confine herself to dogmas deduced from the natural moral law. But this was not the Council's way. From the discussion in St. Peter's during the third session of the Council there emerged a more or less successful aim, put forward by the Commission as the clear intention of the Council majority. This aim was that, together with all the emphasis that was to be laid on elements shared in common (with particularly careful reference to truths which are accessible to reason) and with the constant endeavor to speak a language comprehensible to all, *everything should be clearly considered in the light of the Gospel.*

The final reason for this important decision is this: the Gospel outlook is intended by God for all men: all have a right to insist that the Church

10

should adopt this attitude towards them and should trust them to understand it, for it is not essentially strange to them provided it be open and up-to-date. Furthermore, the Church must present herself in all sincerity if she wishes in her essential capacity as a Church to enter into a dialogue with men. To do this she must reveal herself with all those qualities which are peculiarly her own.

This decision of the Council, to deal with everyone and everything from the point of view of the Gospel, the Church's own unique possession, and to make this Gospel as far as possible accessible to all, is sure to exercise a great influence over the further development of the doctrine of natural moral law. In the future it will be expanded and explored *within the law of Christ*, and not as something apart from this. All is to be judged in the light of the Gospel, but without refraining from a courageous use of human reason and a frank dialogue with all men.

Gaudium et Spes is not an indication that the Church has entered into some sort of "promised land" as the press at times reported. It is nevertheless an important signpost erected by the Church of the Second Vatican Council on the way which leads into a new era. Those elements which guide us into the future must now be brought fully into the light and developed by theology so that the faith of all

God's people may render them fruitful. In its whole conception *Gaudium et Spes* is a constructive and comprehensive answer to the complex problems presented by Communism. If Christians, and with them all men of good will, follow the directives laid down by this Constitution, Communism will lose its appeal, and its best disciples will follow new lines of thought, full of hope for the future.

I shall mention here only the most important points:

Unlike the exponents of Collectivism, with its tendencies towards de-personalization, the Pastoral Constitution lays great stress on the worth of the individual and of freedom, and on his personal responsibility towards society.

The essence of Individualism, which is also very popular among Christians and which helped Communism into power, is discredited when men reach a full understanding of the universality of salvation, a universality which should embrace all earthly things.

Marxism, as a philosophy of history, was able to seduce men who only knew Christianity as a collection of abstract, unhistorical theses. In opposition to this, Vatican II presents a thoughtful study of the history of salvation, which is likewise reflected in a Christian anthropology that takes into serious consideration the historical truth about men in every sphere of life.

A theology which includes all terrestrial things and activities, and is obviously well grounded in doctrine, refutes the Marxists' assertion that Christianity estranges us from our obligations as members of human society. The Council succeeds in arousing those energies which enable the Christian to work for justice and brotherly love, with a sense of social responsibility which leaves the Marxist far behind.

The logical result of the development of man's whole vocation in economic activity, in the search for wisdom and in worship reveals the stark poverty of dialectical materialism which tries to explain everything from the point of view of *homo faber*, the "working man."

The Constitution's new and characteristic treatment of marriage and the family, culture, economics, politics and peace among nations refutes one by one all the main errors of Marxism, with its substructure and superstructure of doctrine, while at the same time certain valid demands latent in Marxism or presented in a distorted way take their rightful place in the Christian life.

Chapter 2

The Council and Communism

In the Council documents we read about the men who declare themselves to be atheists. They assert their atheism so energetically and systematically that they give the impression that it is a kind of faith. The atheist wishes to build up a complete system in absolute freedom, in order to prove that this freedom of his is of the greatest possible value. A typical exponent of this postulatory atheism was Nicolai Hartmann, a Professor of Philosophy at the State University of Berlin before and during Hitler's rule. He postulated the necessity of atheism as a condition for moral freedom: according to him a man could by means of this freedom succeed in constructing or selecting his own moral system of values in complete independence. The Council considers that the consciousness of power aroused in man by modern technical progress can lend the necessary coloring to such a doctrine. This type of modern human being is convinced that he is not laboring in vain when he helps to build a modern tower of Babel, and tries to storm the heights of heaven. National Socialism was a form of this systematic atheism built on human pride.

Finally the Council speaks of the strongest and most powerful manifestation of atheism in the history of mankind: dialectical materialism, which "expects the liberation of man to come about through his economic and social emancipation." [3] This is a belligerent form of atheism. The Synod avoids speaking of it as a "Communist" form, because not all advocates of Communism or of the total socialization of economic life believe in this militant atheism. But the Council presents a clear picture of historical development when it says: "Consequently, when the exponents of this doctrine take over the government of a country they fight very vigorously against religion. They promote atheism by using those means of pressure which public power has at its disposal. This is especially the case in the work of educating the young." [4] Above all the Council denounces the misuse of political power seen in the attempt to force this atheism into the whole system of education.

WHY NO CONDEMNATION?

But why has the Council avoided issuing any outright condemnation of Communism? Towards the end of the Council the well organized group of conservative bishops (*Coetus Internationalis Patrum*) tried quite openly and with all the means at their disposal to obtain such a condemnation. They even asserted that only the disloyalty of a few secretaries prevented the Council from condemning the whole Communist system. But this was by no means the case.

On several occasions the theological commission had debated this theme, and there were various reasons why they did not submit a proposal for a condemnation of Communism by the whole Council. The chief reasons were probably the following:

1. The Council had already prepared the text of paragraphs 20 and 21 of the *Pastoral Constitution on the Church in the Modern World*, in which the existence and causes of atheism were explicitly deplored. The strongest disapproval was expressed with regard to those atheists who misused their economic and political power for ideological purposes. If at this particular moment the Council had aligned itself with that group and issued a solemn condemnation of Communism, then other people besides the Communists themselves would have said that this had been done with an eye on the next political elections in Italy or for some other political purpose. The impression would have been given that the Church had made use of religion to further its political aims. Therefore, in the eyes of our contemporaries, the main issue would have seemed to be not the condemnation of atheism as a denial of religion but rather the rejection of a political system.

2. If the Council had decided to condemn Communism it would have been bound to distinguish very carefully between its various

14

forms. It would have been senseless to condemn only the historical forms of dialectical materialism, without casting a glance at its more recent developments. The attitudes of Communist philosophers and of the various Communist governments show a great diversity. We see already certain indications of future forms of Communism which will refuse to identify themselves with this systematic atheism.

3. The chief aim of paragraphs 19-21 was not a forthright condemnation of atheism — which is and remains condemned — but rather an attempt to find the hidden reasons for this denial of God. In other words: the Christian Church needed to probe its conscience. The insertion of a solemn condemnation of Communism might have been a pretext for avoiding this necessary self-examination. But the Council accepted the challenge of Communism. "Taken as a whole, atheism is not a spontaneous growth, but stems from a variety of causes, including a critical reaction against religious beliefs and in some places against the Christian religion in particular. Therefore believers may be said to have had their share of responsibility for the birth of atheism. In so far as they neglect their own education in the faith or teach erroneous doctrine, or are deficient in their religious, moral, or social life, they must be said to

conceal rather than reveal the authentic face of God and of religion." [5]

4. The Council sets out to provide a constructive answer to the problems presented by the new forms of atheism. The future of the Church, especially of its theological studies and its educational tasks, will be conditioned by the necessity of effectively preaching the Gospel to those who are infected or endangered by modern atheism.

MAIN LINES FOR FUTURE RESEARCH

(a) New emphasis is laid on man's worth as a religious being. The value of freedom too is strongly stressed. It becomes clear that the admirable freedom of God's sons and daughters does not allow them to enslave anyone. The religious ideal of freedom must be reflected in all human relationships. Not only religious and moral instruction, but the Church also in her own right as a teaching Church, must strengthen and set forth in a clearer light this exalted ideal of man's worth and of his freedom.

(b) The unbelief of the modern world often presents a mixture of pride and despair. The faithful, and especially all who preach the faith, must carefully eschew arrogance and any

15

God did not create man as a solitary. no. 12

other form of cowardice. The search for religious truth and its expression must always be continued in full awareness of the fact that we cannot see God face to face. But gratitude to God, who reveals himself in so many wonderful ways, is an essential element of Christian faith and witness.

(c) Whereas dialectical materialism to a certain extent represents a strong reaction against those Christians who, under the cloak of religion, defend the old "established" but unjust order, or have neglected their proper duties in the economic and social spheres, the Council shows that Christian hope, mindful of salvation won for us long ago, directs our energies to the world around us. Belief and hope induce the Christian to make use of all human and religious resources in an attempt to build a better world, that is, to promote genuine brotherhood on all planes. It will be the chief task of future educators of "adult" Christians to make it clear that the liturgy and all other religious activities have to prove their validity by their fruits, because the believer must above all else seek social justice, peace and love. For the sake of truth we must add that the absence of a religious spirit and a total lack of faith have in the past often been deleterious to human dignity and to genuine social relationships. We must not forget Hitler, Stalin and Mao Tse-Tung. These

17

men should serve as a warning to all who wish to construct a world society without God.

(d) Everyone should be concerned about whether all human beings are assured of enough space, time and spiritual energy to be able to reflect on the great problems of mankind, the enigma of life and the origin and destination of man.

(e) Religious doctrine and practice should be presented in such a way that religion becomes more closely involved in life, and life more intimately penetrated with the religious spirit, and of course religion must present a true worship of the living God. This is impossible unless we feel a reverent admiration for man, in whom the glory of God is reflected. The Church can help people to overcome their disbelief only to the extent that, in her official manifestations as in the lives of her members, she is seen to be an ever more visible proof of the presence of the living and loving God among men. Mere arguments, without the authentic witness of love, remain ineffective and in fact frequently produce the contrary result.

(f) The Council preaches not only peaceful co-existence between believers and non-believers, but also a common effort to create a better world. This is necessary for world peace, as Pope John in his Encyclical *Pacem in Terris* clearly demonstrated. This much-to-be desired collaboration presupposes the presence of Christians who have come of age and who are capable of the "discerning of spirits." The Council insists that there can be no fruitful co-operation without a dialogue which must be as sincere and frank as it is shrewd and learned. The co-operation of genuine Christians with agnostics or even with atheists can be the most effective means of inducing all sincere men to think seriously about religious questions, and even about faith itself.

The Young Christian Workers' Movement has shown that many young workers who at first had no religious faith at all were able to find explicit faith in the one God and Father of all mankind through working in collaboration with genuinely Christian Youth Workers. This will happen more and more frequently when we have more Christians who have made a profound study of their faith, who know the conditions of our life today and have found ways of bearing a worthy witness to their faith before this modern world.

Chapter 3

World Concepts, Holy and Profane

The various forms of morality and asceticism
are decisively conditioned by the various implicit
or explicit world concepts, which on their
part are conditioned by the various meanings
given to the term "holiness." Here one should
perhaps remember the lines from Horace (*Ode
to Licinius*), which so characteristically
expresses the pagan point of view:

What man soe'er the golden mean doth choose,
Prudent will shun the hovel's foul decay;
But with like sense, a palace will refuse
And vain display.

The Pastoral Constitution on the Church in the
Modern World is concerned with the problems
of the "hovel" as well as those of the "palace."
It makes a determined attempt clearly to
define what is meant by a world concept that
is truly "global," and in so doing it draws
attention to the variety and multiplicity of human
experience: "Therefore the Council focuses
attention on the world of men, the whole human
family together with all those realities in the
midst of which that family lives. It gazes
upon that world which is the stage on which
man's history has evolved, and which bears
the marks of his endeavors, his tragedies and his
triumphs, that world which the Christian sees

as created and sustained by its Maker's love, which fell into the bondage of sin but is now reedemed by Christ. He was crucified and rose again to break the stranglehold of the Evil One, so that this world might be remade according to God's design and attain its fulfillment." [6]

CREATION OF THE GOOD GOD

The starting point of a Christian world concept will always be the sublime vision of the first chapter of Genesis and of the first chapter of St. John's Gospel. The world is more than a mere thing or creature: it is a word which comes to us through the loving power of the Word of God; it is a message from God to man, for whose sake all visible things were made.

Man comes to an understanding of himself and of the world by listening to the message and the call which he hears in his innermost being and also in the midst of his life among his fellows. He is "the only creature on earth that God willed for his own sake, and he cannot fully find himself except through sincere self giving." [7]

He is therefore not truly human if he isolates himself like an encapsulated atom. He becomes his true self when he is responsive to God and to the human community and feels radically united with the whole universe. When he is thus responsive he receives the message of divine love and awakens to a consciousness of his own existence. He will truly become the image of God when he recognizes himself and everything else as a reflection of the power and love of God.

Everything is the gift of the God of the Holy Trinity who desires to share his love with man, *condiligentes se* (Duns Scotus). The world is a grand process, in which light and darkness are separated one from the other so that finally all may become fully conscious of that which impels them to be their true selves, in conscious self-surrender and worship. The world is all that has happened in the past and is still happening, and is kept in being by God alone, but man is in the midst of the world as a co-active, worshiping, attentive and responsive partner. He remains in this sacred central position and post of honor by virtue of his humble adoration of God and by the progressive development and revelation of his capacity for loving. It is said of this world: "And God saw everything that he had made and behold, it was very good" (Gn 1:31).

The theological works of Teilhard de Chardin are written in modern language in praise of the glory of creation, just as the Psalms are an expression of piety in the

characteristic language of the civilization of their day. This praise must always be expressed in a truly Christian morality. The world which God has entrusted to man and which includes our own human nature as a prototype, is a miraculous world. Because of the dynamic presence of God in it, it invites men to investigate and discover more and more of its latent possibilities of good for man.

Theism, and particularly the doctrine of creation found in the Bible, grant man a wide berth of freedom in his capacity as a wise steward of the natural world. No area should be denied his interest or barred from his concern. Nothing should impede his efforts on behalf of the welfare and genuine progress of mankind. When this suggests or requires the modification of the "nature" of created things, including that of human biological structures, he should be limited only by his respect for human life and the laws of his Creator. Man who is made in the image and likeness of God (Gn 1:27) has, even in his state of dependence upon him, a certain share in his continuing work of creation.

ENSLAVED BY CORRUPTION

His own nature and the whole universe around him are a perpetual invitation to man to thank God and to worship him, to praise him in all his works, and especially by a loyal compliance with the loving intentions of his Creator who has ordained everything for his good. As long as man is absorbed in himself — in a monologue with the "old serpent" — and refuses to offer thanks to God (Gn 3), he will become for himself, his fellow men and in a certain sense for the whole world a source of pride and vanity, thwarting his Creator's plan.

"For although they knew God they did not honor him as God or give thanks to him, but they became futile in their thinking, and their senseless minds were darkened" (Rm 1: 21). The world is intended to rise to full self-consciousness in man through that worship of God which teaches us the greatest consideration, respect and love for our fellows and uses all created things for the good of all mankind. In his self-absorption man frustrates, in so far as he is able, the true humanization of the world and so prevents the glorification of God. "For the creation waits with eager longing for the revealing of the sons of God; for the creation was subjected to futility, not of its own will, but by the will of him who subjected it in hope" (Rm 8:19-20).

Whenever man is a true worshiper of God, and only in so far as his worship is sincere, the earth is blessed with God's presence. "They heard the sound of the Lord God walking in the evening in the cool of the day" (Gn 3:8). The man who worships God respects his fellow man as an image and likeness of God and in so doing he finds the purpose of all things.

The self-absorbed man does not pray; neither does he respect his neighbor as a person. He completely fails to understand the most profound meaning of all created things; he does not recognize them as gifts from God or as objects to be held in trust for God. He does not transform them into a vehicle of loving service; he thwarts the purpose of the whole created world. The biblical doctrine of creation and sin makes it exceedingly clear that sin does not only concern the invisible soul of man: it throws man's whole environment into disorder. And this disordered environment has great power to corrupt man unless, with all his energies and in co-operation with all the good endeavors of other men, he does his best to humanize the world around him. Man cannot remain free unless, as an individual and as a member of a community, he makes good use of his freedom in this world.

The individual who is concerned merely with saving his own lambs from drowning, the man who runs away from the world and thinks only of his own salvation, betrays the world: he himself is "worldly" in the derogatory sense of the word. He not only impoverishes himself by burying his talent: he also spreads vanity and frustration all around him.

OBJECT OF GOD'S MERCY

The Bible teaches us no abstract theory about inherited sin and the sinful world. It speaks of sin only in an existential context. The sinful world in all its misery is the object of God's compassion. It receives the offer and the appeal of his mercy. It is hopelessly sinful only in so far as it refuses this offer and shuts itself up in heartless indifference. Man is never simply a passive victim. In all that he suffers from the vanity and heartlessness of his environment he is always the object of God's redeeming love, if he will but humbly accept this offer. "For God so loved the world that he gave his only Son, that whoever believed in him should not perish but have eternal life. For God sent the Son into the world, not to condemn the world, but that the world might be saved through him" (Jn 3: 16-17).

Christ shows a particular preference for the poor and for all who have been exploited, and for those who have become aware of their own misery and sinfulness. He is the Redeemer of all who cry to him in their sin and who suffer in a sinful, heartless environment. The fruits of redemption are seen in those who have shown mercy and compassion.

Christ does not redeem only man's soul, he redeems the whole man, man in his world. He is the "Savior of the world." The original plan of creation and of redemption in Christ gave man an urgent task to perform, and the duty to exercise a healing influence in the world. According to the degree in which he thankfully responds to God's mercy, he will try to understand the yearning of all men and of all creation; he will have pity on their fear and anguish and in his newly won freedom he will, to the extent of his talents and capacities, co-operate in the construction of a more human and brotherly world.

The doctrine of inherited sin and of the sinful world can, as we said, only be understood, in a Christian context, in its categorical existential significance: no one can withdraw himself from the degrading influences of his environment unless he preaches Christ's merciful love for the world and, to the best of his ability, brings the light of truth, the warmth

of love and the spirit of responsibility into the world around him. No one is handed over, a helpless victim, to the powers of evil and the bitter frustrations of the world if he accepts and preaches Christ's loving and redeeming union with all men and with the whole world.

All lamentations about the sinfulness of the world are nonsensical and un-Christian, even anti-Christian, unless we have given serious thought to the power of redemption and to the fact that it is man's duty to love the world with a healing and saving devotion. All who believe in creation and redemption and struggle to create a healthier environment and who even to some extent pledge their own freedom in this struggle are, because of this effort on behalf of their fellows, more easily capable of feeling a liberating joy when they observe all the good that is intermingled with their sinful environment.

In their gratitude they will become more and more the heralds and agents of God's mercy. The freedom of God's children, which is a gift of the divine mercy, shows itself repeatedly to be our Redeemer's answer to the yearning of all created things to share in this very freedom (cf. Rm 8).

SACRALIZED NATURE

Beginning with the primitive forms of animism
and continuing our research until we come
to the characteristic "fertility cults," we find a
"sacralization" of the world which in practice
subjects man to impersonal world forces and
the course of events. This false sacralization
produces a mass of laws and taboos which are
obstacles to man's genuine progress. The
belief in a personal God and Creator,
reappearing in full purity in Christ, frees man
from this worship of the world and from
imprisonment in it. "If with Christ you died to
the elemental spirits of the universe, why
do you live as if you still belonged to the world?
Why do you submit to regulations: 'Do not handle,
Do not taste, Do not touch'?" (Col 2:
20-22).

The glorification of man's works is quite
different from the sacralization or
idolization of the processes of nature. When the
Bible warns us against idolatry it does not mean
merely the adoration of the bit of wood
or gold from which a household god has been
fashioned; it is rather a much more
general warning to man not to make his own
work or cultural achievements, or the power
of the State, his final aim. Whenever the
prophets preach against Babel and Egypt they
are not merely showing their disapproval
of a worldly state, even as opposed to a
theocracy: they are preaching against the
idolization of a state civilization and of
political power. It is a warning to Israel herself
not to aim at national power but to surrender
herself completely to God. Jesus withdraws
himself from those who seek to make him an
earthly king, since all their hope is centered in
earthly power and greatness. In sharp contrast
to any identification of the Messianic hope with
the privileges and ascendancy of particular
groups or of a particular nation, Jesus
announces the kingdom of heaven, God's own
kingdom, the liberating sovereignty of the
all-embracing love of God. The length and
breadth, height and depth, of God's love
revealed in Christ liberate man from an
idolatrous cult of the world and in so doing
actually set the world and all man's creative
work in its proper worldly and human context.

HOPELESS AND CONDEMNED

The world in its most negative and hopeless
sense was in fact, in St. John's Gospel, not the
secularized world but the ecclesiastical clique
which had become an end to itself, the priests and
Pharisees who wished to make a good living
and a title to power out of their religion.

That "world" for which in the end Jesus ceased to pray (Jn 17:9) was not that of worldly politicians, prostitutes, tax gatherers or circus folk, but the world of those "religious circles" who self-righteously considered themselves superior to all others and coveted the highest rank and most pompous titles, always in the name of religion. Unspiritual religious "works," spiritual pride, the exploitation of spiritual office to satisfy vanity and the lust for power are much more hostile to God, much more truly the "sinful world," than any earthly civilization and power set up as an idol. Worldliness masquerading as religion has a more repellent effect than any other form of idolatry. The clique of priests and Pharisees who brought Christ to the Cross is simply the image of that "world" which shuts God out. Christ did everything he could to arouse and shock this world which glorifies itself; in resisting his grace it has become unregenerate. This world, clothed in sacred vestments, which shows its blindness most clearly in its attitude to the revelation of God's holiness in Christ, has at the same time — always in the name of its sacred rules — lost all compassion for its fellow men. These are the men who slander Christ because he heals on the Sabbath day.

The first letter of St. John identifies the "godless world" with those people who dishonor God the Father of all because they do not show any love towards their fellow men (cf. 1 Jn 3:10). It is impossible for man, who seeks for salvation, to believe in God, the Father of all, if he hates God's children, mankind, that is, if he does not feel any love for them. Brotherly love makes us God's family, whereas lovelessness signifies the "world outside" which is ignorant of salvation. By accepting brotherly love as the greatest gift and supreme rule, "we know that we are of God, and the whole world is in the power of the evil one" (1 Jn 5: 19).

The most frequently quoted text about the "evil world" is a pointer in the same direction: "Do not love the world or the things in the world. If anyone loves the world, the love for the Father is not in him. For all that is in the world, the lust of the flesh and the lust of the eyes and the pride of life, is not of the Father but is of the world" (1 Jn 2: 15-16). It is obvious that the world which has been condemned is not the external world, as contrasted with man's inner world, or even as contrasted with a sphere of life which has been considered to be a sacred domain, but is instead a mental attitude which naturally also determines the external forms of life and of the world.

CARNAL AND PROFANE

In the first Epistle of St. John the negatively defined "world" concept is expressed not so much with reference to a category of priests who isolated themselves from their fellow men as with reference to the Gnostics who conceded validity only to the unsubstantial ideas of their own philosophy and despised the body, as indeed they despised all visible and tangible things. They denied the incarnation of God. Contempt of the visible world led them to this rejection of the Word made flesh. The apostate Christians who became "prophets" of Gnosticism joined forces with "the evil world." "By this you know the Spirit of God: every spirit which confesses that Jesus Christ has come in the flesh is of God, and every spirit which does not confess Jesus is not of God. This is the spirit of Antichrist, of which you heard that it was coming, and now it is in the world already" (1 Jn 4:1-3). In this passage St. John refers to those who despised the created world, particularly the world of the flesh, as belonging to the "world," that is, as people hostile to Christ. Contempt of the flesh is one of the grossest forms of profane worldliness, which is the same as unregenerate unworldliness.

In the same sense, the Apostle of the Gentiles attacks on the one hand the self-righteousness of the legalists and on the other hand presumptuousness of the Greek philosophers who rejected the actual death of Jesus on the cross and the Christian belief in the resurrection of the body. The refusal to accept with due respect the body and the good things of this world is a characteristic of the "evil world." This attitude robs creatures of any motive to praise God.

A "HOLY" WORLDLINESS

The profane worldliness of the Pharisees reveals itself as a nefarious attempt to sever religion from life. In fact they took away the divine element from real life in the world, from human relationships and from our relationship with the natural world. In contrast with such tendencies, which have survived even until our own day, we now speak of "holy worldliness" in the traditional sense, namely, of that holiness which through the whole created world gives honor to God. A "holy worldliness" is an expression of liberation from man's egotism and self absorption, a liberation also from that sterile sacralization which constructs a "holy" domain, from which to all intents and purposes the social order of the world, its culture and

To encourage and stimulate
cooperation among men, the Church
must be thoroughly present in
the midst of the community
of nations.   no. 89

politics, are excluded. But at the same time
holy worldliness also means freedom from any
idolization of the world. It is essentially that
spirit of freedom with regard to the world
which springs from a close union with God and
from the love felt for every human being.

Holy worldliness is the worship of God in
the spirit, and in the truth of our
human life; it is a vital response to all the ways
in which God reveals his creative power and
love. Holy worldliness hears the Canticle of
the Sun sung by all God's creatures and interprets
it, above all, as an expression of gratitude
and of the thankful acceptance of all the
possibilities God offers us for serving our
fellows. Holy worldliness sees in everyone and
everything a message, a ray of God's love, and
is used by man freely and adoringly as an
expression of brotherly and responsible love.
This service of love in our present condition
becomes a worshipful response to God.

Holy worldliness abolishes the artificial,
sharply defined frontiers between the sacred
and the profane which have been set up by an
all too self-conscious clique of priests or by
ascetics who despise the world. It restores the
glory of divine creation to the body and to
material substance by a prayerful response to
all the ways in which God reveals himself. Holy
worldliness liberates the energies of the heart

29

and will from all ceremonial scrupulosity, to make room for belief in the living God and for love for our fellows, to be expressed in the conditions of our daily life. It raises real life with all its heights and depths to God in prayer. It speaks the actual language of life in the liturgy and in theology. It does not wait until words and melodies have acquired an archaic character before it consents to use them as sacred language and music. All that here and now is most full of life is harvested in faith and ennobled, deepened and purified in worship. Therefore worship which expresses itself in living forms will be reflected in our daily lives.

Holy worldliness gives its appropriate value to explicit prayer and meditation, to prayerful readings of Holy Scripture and to the glorification of God's work for our redemption. Without explicit prayer, life will not develop into the worship of God in spirit and in truth. Genuine prayer raises real life to God and leads us back once more to a fuller appreciation and mastery of life in the light of faith. Holy worldliness includes contemplation, but contemplation with all five senses. It is a wondering acceptance of God's visible revelation of himself; it is a final assent to the mystery of the Incarnation: "That which was from the beginning, which we have heard, which we have seen with our eyes, which we have looked

upon and touched with our hands, concerning the Word of life . . ." (1 Jn 1:1).

Holy worldliness demands a liturgy which shall make the Christian fully aware of his mission in the world. True worldliness is unable to say "Our Father" without feeling enthusiasm for the service of all God's children.

Holy worldliness needs an existential theology, a glorification of God's work in the history of mankind, a theology which is prepared to consider the actual existential problems of men in the light of the "Good News," and which proclaims the new life in Christ, which is always a life in the service of our fellow men, in the language and intimacy of the spirit of our own times — but without succumbing to the impurities of the age.

The doctrine of the sacramental nature of marriage is a classical example of holy worldliness. The history of this doctrine, however, offers many examples of the constant danger of severing religion from life. The Council of Trent teaches that the grace of the Sacrament, which Christ won through suffering, "perfects the natural love of the husband and wife, strengthens their indissoluble unity and thereby sanctifies the marriage partners themselves." [8] Therefore it is clear that genuine holiness and a state of grace in

30

marriage are present when the husband and wife love each other in a truly human, tender and passionate way and are loyally devoted to each other.

Artificial sacralism, estranged from life, concentrates all its attention on the contract and its validity, and the ceremonial aspect of marriage, explaining that marital love is a matter of merely secondary importance. It commends a purely supernatural love of God and neighbor, and asserts that the marital union is only free from sin in so far as it is used merely for the procreation of children or in so far as it represents a *remedium concupiscentiae* (a remedy against concupiscence) and so is a lesser evil than unchastity. In *Gaudium et Spes* the Second Vatican Council explicitly asserts that the whole of married life is included in the sacrament. The married pair glorify God in the wholeness of their love, in a truly human manner.

The primary sacramental symbols link the Christian liturgy with the full flow of human life and give the believer a chance to enjoy a redeemed existence, which shall glorify God in a truly human way. The eucharist portrays the suffering, death and resurrection of the Lord, and therefore signifies the heavenly feast of love which unites us all. But this should be regarded primarily as the symbol of a family meal. The Mass, heavily overladen with Byzantine court ceremonial, in which the priest turned his back on the people, separated from them by the iconostasis, or was at least very far removed from them in his own "holy" separate sphere with a "holy" language which the people could not understand, became to some extent a symbol of the barrier between religion and life, a barrier between the consecrated priest and the "unholy" people. One must admit that the highly developed clerical liturgy of recent centuries was far removed from the simplicity of the Last Supper at which Christ was united with his disciples around a table, washed their feet, answered their questions and actually shared their repast.

The liturgy is one of the means Christ uses to teach his people the great commandment of love. Its renewal went much further than the initial translation of the Eucharistic rite from a "holy" (because dead) language. Its whole structure was revitalized to provide a renewed understanding and a renewed form of expression which would enable those who take part in it to be more fully aware of the fact that redemption does not estrange them from real life but rather sends them out to work for the salvation of all their fellows. In addition, it is a function of the liturgy to make it clear to us that salvation depends finally not on earthly achievements but on the grace of God, and on the intervention of his saving love. But the assent to grace is essentially an acceptance of the existing possibilities of making Christ's love known to our fellows.

The liturgy, considered purely as a "cult," had separated itself from the experience of life, from living language and living music, and had become strictly circumscribed with many binding regulations with regard to sacred vestments, consecrated stones and holy ceremonies. It no longer made a truly meaningful contact with the world, or showed the way to redemption in ordinary everyday life. A liturgy which had become sterile because it was far too "holy," (meaning "holy" in the false sense) had its counterpart in a sterile theology, which had likewise remained imprisoned not only in a dead language but also in the definitions of outworn philosophies and in the problems of bygone times as the result of a falsely interpreted orthodoxy. Since it was "un-worldly" in the sense that it avoided all environmental problems concerned with everyday life, it removed God from the world and kept him, too, estranged from the actual substance of our life.

In truly prophetic indignation Karl Marx opposed those forms of religiosity which were known to him, which on the one hand ratified the *status quo* of the privileged classes and on the other hand failed to arouse any vital energies for the reforming of men's lives. He raged against a narrow view of individual salvation which expressed itself in "pure" religious consolations and scruples, while the new economic and social developments were greatly endangering the chances of salvation for the working masses. In opposition to this, Marx offered an integral concept of existence based on the fundamental consideration of the whole function of man in the economic sphere from which he expected man's integral future development. In this alone was his massive world-religion completely opposed to integration into the great prophetic tradition of Israel which reached its climax in Christ. The Old Testament prophets and Christ himself, agree with him in condemning that sacralization of a sterile cult which estranged man from life and set up a formalistic clerical caste. But Christ and the prophets were inspired by a zeal for God's honor, a zeal which directs all the energies aroused by worship to the service of one's fellow men with their very real contemporary problems.

HOPE OF THE WORLD TO COME

In announcing the kingdom of heaven, Christ promised us eternal salvation. But we must try to have a clear concept of the world to come: the kingdom of God is not built on any human claims or achievements. It does not encourage the worldly ambitions of powerful and privileged people, and is absolutely opposed to any idolization of culture and politics. It is a promise independent of external and visible success and is not concerned with human prowess. The kingdom of God lies in eternity, beyond the short span of our earthly life: it means eternal life with God.

Nevertheless, the kingdom of God has truly appeared in our own lives, visibly and tangibly, with the coming of the incarnate Word of God. It has assumed a human form in the humility, love and kindness of Christ who bears the burdens of all men and directs everything to God's glory. The soul which abandons itself entirely to Christ, the Anointed One, is already united with all the redeemed as an earnest of the redemption of the whole human race. It is as if all creation had been waiting to enjoy the first fruits of redemption in Christ's disciples, and now to some extent actually shares in these. Already, here on earth, the family of the redeemed can do the will of

God, "as in heaven," if they love him. The expectation of salvation "in the world to come" is based wholly and exclusively on what God has already revealed. When we believe in God's work of salvation we already see the outlines of the new heaven and the new earth.

Our hope is not in liberation from the prison of the flesh but in the resurrection of the body; not the joy of individual souls but a joyful union in the glorification of our love for the Holy Trinity, in communion with the saints, and in universal brotherly charity. By glorifying God's work of redemption and enjoying the hope which urges us onwards, our present obligations and possibilities of salvation are not only not diminished but are enriched with the greatest possible profundity and significance. A "cult" Christianity which excludes the hope of eternity is not truly Christian: it will always degenerate into expectations similar to those of the German "Christians" of the Third Reich. It will not be through any diminishment of our hope for eternal life that we will liberate our energies for service to our fellow men and to the world of today and give us a sense of responsibility for future generations. But we must have a true understanding of eschatological hope. Since Christian hope is based on the fully visible union of Christ with all men and

all creatures and aims at universal brotherhood, we find a practical expression of our gratitude and of our expectation in our present obligation to work for increased human solidarity and brotherliness, justice and righteousness.

The Pastoral Constitution *Gaudium et Spes* has explicitly put forward not only a religion which is open to the world around us — a holy worldliness — but also its solid foundation in eschatological hope. It is not a diminishment but rather a deeper understanding and a totally consistent concept of hope which gives to our sense of present responsibility and to our loving provision for future generations their full meaning as a preparation for universal brotherhood.

The "expectation of salvation" of traditional Marxism is a false transcendentalism. One cannot expect total brotherliness while one asserts class hatred as a duty and fundamental obligation, as a norm of the present world. On the contrary, the Christian believes that love, to be perfected only in eternity, is already powerfully at work and eager to use all its energies in neighborly service. Since love has become visible in Christ and has taken on our human flesh, the Christian knows it is his duty to express his faith and hope, and his sanctification by the Holy Spirit, in the realities of his daily life: he knows he must be involved in the visible world, but without becoming its slave.

Learned treatises about the divine virtue of hope, written from the point of view of dogmatic and moral theology, certainly need re-writing with fuller and more profound treatment of those aspects which help us to attain a clearer understanding of the present hour and a serious consideration of our duties to the world around us. Hope in the life to come must free itself from those elements which, instead of opening men's hearts to the great and genuinely human reality of love, uselessly absorb or impede a large proportion of their energies. For example, the emphasis on individual salvation to the exclusion of interest in the salvation of others is not conducive to the true welfare of the whole human family, even when it is motivated by the desire for a more human order of existence and a wiser use of all earthly possibilities. A one-sided or over-developed concentration on the "valid" administration and "valid" reception of the sacraments as a necessary condition for salvation, in which validity was treated as something quite apart from any manifestation of faith and hope, misdirected valuable energies into a blind alley.

AUTONOMY OF SECULAR ENTERPRISE AND SCIENCE

In a long struggle and with a great effort modern culture has lost its clerical character and become worldly and secular, freeing itself from every vestige of ecclesiastical authority. It undoubtedly still owes gratitude to the clerics for their achievements, particularly those of the monastic Orders. Without the Church Europe would presumably have sunk into the barbarism during the transition from the centuries of antiquity to the Middle Ages. It was however unfortunate that the cleric made a monopoly of a service which he certainly intended to offer, in a paternalistic manner, for the good of the world. Naturally there were even then some resolute pioneers who adopted a freer attitude to modern science, and some champions of lay scholarship even among the ranks of the monks and priests. One need only mention Abelard, or Erasmus of Rotterdam.

The medieval university still took as its model that *universitas scientiarum* in which theology had always reigned supreme. Even its least important pronouncements had the echoes of eternity. Its results and its ways of thinking reflected a lack of thoughtful understanding of the message of salvation and of a true world concept. This failure and other limitations were

Christ was crucified and rose again ... so that this world might be fashioned anew according to God's design.   no. 2

the reason for the fanatical religious preoccupations with the question as to whether the earth revolved around the sun, or the sun around the earth. The case of Galileo was not un-typical of the whole situation. At the time of the Vatican Council it had become obvious that the wheel has turned full circle.

Theology no longer claims to dictate, any more than the Papacy claims a *potestas directa in temporalia*, direct power in temporal affairs. Earthly spheres are now independent of theology and of ecclesiastical authority. In this sense they are secularized; they are known and recognized in their autonomy. But the individual man who is involved with them is still subject to God, no less than he was in medieval times. Faith and theology are integrating forces. Theology brings everything under the believer's roof, but does not try to impose a "sacred" and arbitrary solution, such as was for a long time imposed in the question of the prohibition of usury. A theology which is genuinely interested in the world first studies the significance of usury in the secular society and in the economic order before it hazards a religious verdict. The composition of the papal commission for the study of population problems and responsible parenthood is characteristic of this new approach, even if it is not yet obligatory for all

37

theologians to listen first to what the psychologist, biologist, gynecologist and sociologist have to say concerning the entire complex of these questions, before they pronounce a verdict.

By a humble attitude to other sciences theology prepares a careful integration of all spheres of knowledge in the light of faith. Similarly the teachers of Church doctrine are now conscious of their responsibilities and can proclaim the all-encompassing authority of God only in so far as they resist every temptation to gain indirect control over earthly spheres of activity. The theologians and the successors of the Apostles must realize that they can adequately answer questions arising from the complexities of modern life only if they first ascertain (generally through the results of team work) all the available scientific facts.

Theology, as the science of faith, must be aware of the fact that the truth of salvation is declared to us from on high, by divine revelation. But the theologian must also admit that he cannot presume to find out the truth in some superior privileged way of his own, but must always seek it and make use of it by his own efforts "here below," by utilizing all human possibilities. Obedience and faithful adherence to God demand a respectful attitude to all facets of knowledge, no matter who has laboriously discovered them.

The final source of all knowledge is always God himself. The theologian and the ecclesiastic, however, have no monopoly which could allow them to teach a concept of history or a law of nature without first humbly questioning all those available sources of historical knowledge, of psychology and other sciences which have something to say about it.

The Church and ecclesiastical theology can only co-operate with worldly ideologies (which leave no room for God because this would nullify their own achievements) in so far as they are conscientiously aware of the limitations of these ideologies. Holy worldliness demands great humility from all, in order to leave room for him who alone is good.

Chapter 4

Unbelief and the Natural Law

One of the most fundamental problems of theologians today is represented by the vast number of unbelievers in the modern world, and our mission with regard to them.

How can theology play its part in the dialogue with the modern world, in which God sometimes seems no longer present? A more profound study of the natural law could well become an aid not only to missionary endeavor but also to brotherly co-operation among all men of good will, in a common effort to preserve peace on earth.

The natural moral law, which must be carefully distinguished from positive revelation, but also carefully included in a total view of the history of salvation, can to some extent prepare the way for the preaching of the Gospel, if it is considered as a way of speaking about the living God, even when his name is not explicitly mentioned.

Our interpretation of the law of nature was and may still be to some extent a message of bad news, for it implies that since the end of the pre-scientific world, God is dead — dead in our categories and concepts and dead in the hearts of those to whom we offer this doctrine.

Before we consider starting a dialogue with unbelievers about the law of nature we must put forward our own question: What is our attitude, as believers and in the total concept of our faith, to the doctrine of the natural moral law?

Belief in the fullest, most Christian sense is nourished above all by God's Word, his revelation which has its center and fulfillment in Jesus Christ. But it also includes a receptive and attentive attitude to all the other ways in which God reveals his power and love. Faith does not exempt us from making a great effort to understand, with all the powers of our minds and hearts, our task in this world.

Faith, as a response to the revelation of the Word in Christ Jesus, provides us with a profound insight which helps us to adopt the right attitude to moral problems, and particularly to those which are most basic and which most constantly recur. Human experience and this hard-won understanding are however a source of moral knowledge no less for the believer than they are for the unbeliever. In fact they are a greater help to the believer because in the last resort it is only the Christian who knows the more profound significance and value of this knowledge. It leads to more than a merely human understanding: God stands behind it, even if he is sometimes obscured. God speaks through his own creation and above all through man's heart, and through man's own creative work. He tries to communicate with the spirit of man, whom he has created and made responsive for this purpose. As God's creative work is seen in all occurrences and historical developments, so we must try to understand this kind of divine revelation and all human endeavor as an historical process of its own which must however not be considered apart from the history of salvation.

Natural revelation must be sharply distinguished from supernatural revelation because direct divine revelation, which began with "the law and the prophets" and found its fulfillment in Jesus Christ, is a pure gift from God which far surpasses everything that is human and creaturely. But it is also very important to effect an integral union between both types of revelation. There is only one historical plan of salvation. Revelation is integral not only because we have to see Scripture and tradition forming one synthesis, but also because the revelation found in creation must be seen as one with the revelation of the Word. It is the

Children are really
the supreme gift
of marriage.   no. 50

same God who announces his love and purpose for mankind in different ways — to a certain extent through different channels. Revelation and human understanding must not be estranged from each other.

A specifically Christian understanding of the natural moral law does not merely consider the law of Christ and natural law side by side, as two separate entities. For a true synthesis it is all-important that the initial approach should be correct. If in the natural moral law we see only or principally human efforts and achievements, whereas supernatural revelation is understood as God's own manifestation of himself, then the two realities remain on different planes, immured, as it were, on different levels. A theological and characteristically Christian view considers that the natural moral law also originated in God. Its validity is due only to the fact that God is still present in his creation, speaks through it and wishes to be understood. On the other hand, the revelation of the Word requires more than a merely passive acceptance by man: all the resources of his understanding, heart and mind, are needed to comprehend it.

The believer's attitude to the natural law is centered in Christ: "In the beginning was the Word, and the Word was with God, and the Word was God. He was in the beginning with God; all things were made through him, and without him was not anything made that was made" (Jn 1:1-3). The Word in which all things have life and light is the same which became man. Christ is "the image of the invisible God, the firstborn of every creature. For in him all things were created, in heaven and on earth, visible and invisible, whether thrones or dominions or principalities or authorities — all things were created through him and for him. He is before all things, and in him all things hold together" (Col 1: 15-17).

If men are receptive, and hear and understand fundamental religious and moral truths, then not only the basic audibility of the world but also man's own subjective ability to hear proceeds from God the Creator who did not merely wish to construct a world but wished to make himself known through it, and by so doing to communicate with man. The final, recondite meaning of this communion, which became apparent in the fullness of time, is revealed in Jesus Christ, the Word made flesh.

In its most profound intrinsic meaning the natural moral law brings us face to face with the living and loving God. The imperative appeal which rises from the whole work of creation and above all from the depths of man's own heart, is not a collection of abstract rules of conduct but a call to man to worship God, precisely because God wishes to communicate with man.

The natural moral law is pre-eminently a religious reality, but of course one should not therefore claim that everything to do with the natural moral law is meaningless unless its religious basis or religious inspiration is explicitly expressed and acknowledged. "What can be known about God is plain to them, because God has shown it to them. Ever since the creation of the world his invisible nature, namely, his eternal power and deity, has been clearly perceived in the things which have been made. So they are without excuse, for although they knew God they did not honor him as God or give thanks to him" (Rm 1: 19-21).

Consequently, in the believer's attitude towards the natural law the emphasis is placed on God's own actions: He wanted to make himself known to the eyes of reason through his works. This attitude does not encourage any tendency to self-glorification in man, but rather a basic willingness to learn, a readiness to respond. Man must be willing to hear and to respond. Do we not find in this the fundamental structural elements of faith? It is precisely this attitude which makes the Christian receptive to the word of Christ. If we ask whether such an attitude can in itself effect salvation, then the theological answer must refer to Christ: if this attitude is a gift of God's redemptive love then it does mean salvation in Christ, even if the man who is receptive and responsive in this way does not yet know Christ's name.

The believer has a clearer notion of sin than the unbeliever who is similarly receptive to the notion of the natural law. The merely "natural" man does not exist. Sinful men suppress God's truth in various ways. If man's heart is not entirely open to God his understanding also remains somewhat clouded. Redemption brings — among many other graces — a liberating energy for the human reason and an increase of moral strength. In so far as man conquers his selfishness and self absorption by trust in Christ's redemptive acts and the influence of his grace, he acquires a greater sense of personal responsibility and is supported by the whole community of the redeemed. The scales of blindness gradually fall from the eyes of reason. The possibility of discovering all that belongs to the natural moral law leads him to a freer and happier realization of a conscious living faith.

The community of believers, and particularly
the ministers of the Church, consider all the
endeavors of human reason to discover man's
religious and moral mission in this world in the
light and by the judgment of faith. This was
obviously the deliberate intention and attitude
which the Second Vatican Council expressed in
the "Pastoral Constitution on the Church in
the Modern World," and in the "Declaration
on Religious Freedom." Man need neither
forget nor deny the reality of faith in order
to make full use of their reason. They must
of course distinguish between what is a clear
revelation of faith and what they believe they
can discover, by the light of reason, from the
works of creation and even more from
reflecting upon human experience.

It is precisely the full awareness of the
limits of both kinds of experience which
will not only help the believer to avoid
conflicts but also contribute to his existential
unity. The radiance which streams from God's
saving truth, revealed in the living Word, and
an attitude of enlightened faith, create a healthy
atmosphere in which man may exercise his
reason with more hope of success, may
reflect on his moral experience and try to
understand his mission in the world.

DIALOGUE WITH BELIEVERS

Believing Christians and non-Christians can speak together about those realities of the created world which have been made accessible to the eyes of reason (cf. Rm 1:20). We may never exclude the possibility that certain members and groups of non-Christian peoples have developed a deeper and truer understanding of many of the truths of the religious and moral order, which are accessible to reason, than many Christians or Christian groups. We may even find loftier moral principles among non-Christians than in many of our Christian communities. The Church has no monopoly of the natural moral law, although it is part of the sphere of her authentic ministry. A basic condition for useful dialogue is our readiness to learn something from the other participants and to listen to what they have to say before we deliver to them our own message.

A dialogue based on the natural moral law — on those realities and experiences which are accessible to reason — must nevertheless be directed in accordance with the true character of both partners in the discussion. Both partners, Christian as well as non-Christian, will therefore be wise to distinguish very carefully between those theses or speculations which they think they can understand by reason alone, and those truths which they hold only by virtue of their sincere conviction of revelation, or which they accept in absolute loyalty to their religious community. The Christian partner in the dialogue need not conceal his own conception of the relation between the natural moral law and his understanding of his faith. One must avoid both pitfalls, that of the suppression of our own identity and that of the denial of our total conception of truth, and one must not jumble together indistinguishably dogmas of faith and purely rational assertions.

If the ministers of the Church speak of questions concerning the natural moral law, then neither their assumption of a philosophic role nor their reliance on almost 2,000 years of experience, can provide them with sufficient basis for judgment. The essential starting point must be the concept of salvation. But no service is rendered to the cause of salvation either within the confines of the Church or in dialogue with others if the Church relies upon an uncertain or outworn philosophy and is not willing humbly to learn from its own history and from the sum of human experience. It is precisely the control exercised by an enlightened faith which will prevent Christians from asserting more than they can clearly discern, or present to others in a reasonable manner. A dogmatic assertion that a certain thesis is a doctrine arising from the natural moral law is a contradiction in terms unless this thesis can be given a credible foundation. Authority cannot be divorced from basic reason.

DIALOGUE WITH UNBELIEVERS

This rule about preserving separate identities and distinctions must by analogy apply also to the dialogue between believers and unbelievers. In a serious and mutually respectful discussion both partners must know and make known their identities, their points of view and respective attitudes.

Hence there arises the difficult problem: since our way of thinking about the natural moral law reveals a characteristic attitude which, although self-critical, is undeniably that of a believer — that is, receptive to faith — how can we then seize the chance to conduct a dialogue with people whose whole attitude and way of thinking show the characteristics of unbelief? The answer to this question is far from easy. But one thing is clear: hardly ever or anywhere can a sharp line be drawn between black and white. Are there not many Christians — even Christian exponents of the natural law — who

describe themselves as believers on an abstract and institutional plane, but who in many respects, chiefly in their lack of real openness to God's Word and to new discoveries, present some of the characteristic attitudes of unbelief?

On the other hand, there are the various types of the "unconfessed" Christian who defines himself, in the abstract, as an unbeliever but who shows all the fundamental marks of a believer's attitude in his way of living and thinking and also in his way of dealing with questions concerned with the natural moral law. In his constant devotion to moral values and ideals, in his willingness to communicate with his fellows and to appreciate their worth and share their troubles, in his responsiveness to God's call, a response which sets no arbitrary limits to the divine power, his readiness to hear God's message and obey his commands and his selfless devotion to ideals which finally open the door to perfect love, to a perfect Person — do we not see something which may be called implicit faith?

In every serious partner in a dialogue we find at least some signs of such an attitude, something that can serve as a valid bridge; and this becomes all the more likely when we are aware of our own limitations and of our vulnerability to unbelief. Already thinkers like Max

Scheler and Rudolf Otto have taught that
we must not accept an abstract classification as
representing the whole truth. Many a man
professes a pantheistic concept of life and yet
his basic way of thinking is open to an
understanding of the personal God and his
Word.

If we wish to conduct a much needed dialogue
about the natural moral law (including man's
religious disposition of mind) with any
unbeliever, then we must above all make
it clear that our thoughts which are integrated
in our whole attitude to faith, do not impair
our intellectual seriousness and sincerity but on
the contrary stimulate them to the limits of
human possibility. An essential element of this
sincerity is an awareness of the limitations of
our own certainties and uncertainties. Above
all, we must not confuse our personal ideas
with our faith and with the Gospel message.

The "Pastoral Constitution on the Church in
the Modern World" stresses the underlying
organic synthesis as well as this careful
distinction: "Let there be no false opposition
between professional and social activities on
the one hand and religious life on the other . . . .
Christians should rather rejoice in following
the example of Christ, who worked as an artisan.
In the exercise of all their earthly activities
they can gather their humanitarian, domestic,
professional, social and technical enterprises

into one vital synthesis with religious values." [10] It is true that this does not directly refer to the synthesis formed by the confession of faith and considerations of the natural law, but nevertheless it obviously includes also in this connection the attempt to adopt a comprehensive attitude.

Still more explicit is the admonition, in the same section, about making a careful distinction: "Often enough the Christian outlook will itself suggest specific solutions in certain circumstances. Yet it happens rather frequently, and understandably, that with equal sincerity some of the faithful will disagree with others on a given matter. Even against the intentions of their proponents, however, certain solutions proposed by one side or the other may easily be confused by many people with the Gospel message. Hence it is necessary for all to remember that no one is allowed in such situations to appropriate the Church's authority for his own opinion. They should always try to enlighten one another through honest discussion, preserving mutual charity and caring above all for the common good." [11] Only when these basic rules of dialogue are carefully observed within the community of believers will the dialogue with unbelievers also be able to produce good results.

A POSSIBLE CAUSE OF UNBELIEF

The Second Vatican Council had sharp words to say about stubborn unbelief: "Those who willfully shut out God from their hearts and try to evade religious questions are not following the dictates of their consciences, and so they are not free from blame." [12] But whereas on the one hand there are forms of unbelief which in one way or another — often unknown to us — are nevertheless a kind of search for the living God which may be unsuccessful merely because of the obstacles it encounters, on the other hand the Vatican Council admonishes Christians to feel a collective responsibility for this phenomenon of unbelief: "Believers themselves frequently bear some responsibility for this situation. For, taken as a whole, atheism is not a spontaneous growth but stems from a variety of causes, including a critical reaction against religious beliefs, and in some places against the Christian religion in particular. Therefore believers may have had more than a little to do with the rise of atheism. In so far as they neglect their own instruction in the faith, or teach erroneous doctrine, or fail in their religious, moral or social life, they must be said to conceal rather than reveal the authentic face of God and of religion." [13]

The Church "strives to detect in the atheist's

mind the hidden causes for his denial of God. She is aware of the gravity of the questions which atheism raises and, in her love for all men, she believes these questions ought to be more seriously and profoundly examined." [14]

One of the original causes of atheism may be the fear that religion —and especially the doctrine of the natural law proclaimed in the name of religion — does not sufficiently respect the dignity and welfare of the human person and the human community. Some atheists "seem more inclined to glorify man than to deny God." [15] In opposition to these it is particularly necessary to make it clear that the doctrine of the natural moral law is not merely a collection of physical and biological laws (asserted but seldom proved) but in the last resort always concerns "the human being and his behavior," [16] the human community, mutual respect and devotion, the dignity of the individual and genuine brotherliness.

"Man is the only creature on earth which God willed for its own sake." [17] Modern man, especially after his subjection to various tyrannies and to an economic and social system which is to a great extent controlled impersonally, is particularly sensitive to the fact that all things find their moral meaning in the salvation and welfare of the human person and in his relationship with his fellow men. He knows, as the man of the pre-scientific age could not know, that the earth is truly subject to him, which means that he must be a wise controller of all things and all events, even in the biological and psychological spheres, in accordance with the will of God, respect for the dignity of the human person, a more human concept of life and a more complete evolution of the human community.

In this connection there are now signs not only of a new and more responsible study and examination of conscience but above all also of greater reserve and caution. True wisdom must preserve us from simply rejecting all the basic concepts we have hitherto relied on, once we have doubted the validity of the arguments used to support them. Many rules only need to be re-formulated in modern language and in harmony with the new discoveries of science. But sincerity and absolute devotion to the cause of truth and, most of all, the desire to make the Christian message credible, compel us today to be more constantly aware of the limitations of our knowledge of the natural law and of the validity of our arguments, and also to admit these

The livelihood and human dignity of those who are in particularly difficult circumstances because of illness or old age should be safeguarded.   *no. 66*

limitations quite frankly. On the other hand, it is prudent to content oneself, in moral questions, with that degree of certainty which can be genuinely achieved. In this new outlook modern unbelievers of all kinds can help us if we, in humility and with a sense of responsibility, seriously consider their difficulties and their solicitude for certain human values.

THE NATURAL MORAL LAW IN THE SERVICE OF THE GOSPEL

The Second Vatican Council indicates a new direction for the study of natural law which is to be considered as an integral part of the general testimony of God's people. This represents a significant service for the good of all mankind and can strengthen hope and belief in the living God, the Lord of human history. *Pacem in Terris*, Pope John XXIII's great legacy to us, the "Declaration on Religious Freedom" and the "Pastoral Constitution on the Church in the Modern World" were generally understood in this sense. "The Church knows that her message is in harmony with the most secret desires of the human heart when she champions the dignity of the

human vocation, restoring hope to those who have already despaired of anything better than their present lot. Far from diminishing man's dignity, her message brings to his development light, life and freedom." [18]

Today more than ever before the study of the natural law must be based on personal and historical considerations. In God the natural moral law is stated once and for all to be an "eternal law," but a law for the historical man who, it is true, is the same man at all times but nevertheless is conditioned by an everchanging biological, psychological and cultural situation, and with a variable capacity for self-knowledge. The natural law, as far as we can judge, concerns man himself in a particular historical environment and with specific historical possibilities of self-understanding and world understanding. Man acts in harmony with his rational nature when he does all he can in his own circumstances as an individual and as a member of a community to resolve his own problems and those of his age.

Historicity implies for us continuity, but also a discontinuity due to genuine changes and new ways of thought, and to man's adaptation to new circumstances of life and knowledge. Man *is* history, has history and makes history. His historicity is an integral part of his existence and in fact so much so that the whole man shows the characteristics of his time in every feature of his existence, in his intellect, his capacity for love, his humor or lack of it. Historicity implies adaptation to his specifically limited possibilities and a responsible attitude to the future. A deepened understanding of man's historicity is able in its own way to prepare for the message with which Jesus confronted the unbelief of the Sadducees: God is "not the God of the dead, but of the living" (Mt 22:32). An unhistorical abstract approach, with its insensitive, dogmatic component elements, is unable to keep man receptive to faith in the history of salvation or to a super-historical reality; only a sensitive historical approach can do this.

By the term "personalization" I do not mean a self-absorbed individualism, but the personalization of our relationship to God and to our fellow men, and the discovery of our true selves in a state of responsiveness to God and to our fellows. Man "cannot fully find himself except through sincere self-giving." [19] One must not however demand the final or hundredth step from the man who has just started on his way and may give up after the second or third.

One reason for anti-religious unbelief can be found in those "religious" men who feel no urge to establish a world brotherhood but only anxiety for their own salvation, and scrupulously observe an impersonally interpreted natural moral law. The "Pastoral Constitution on the Church in the Modern World" explains that the Christian's eschatological hope, if genuinely and deeply rooted in faith, will be reflected in thoughts and actions which show an awareness of his responsibility towards the whole human community. "This faith needs to prove its fruitfulness by penetrating the believer's whole life, including its worldly dimensions, and by encouraging him to show justice and love, especially to the needy. But what most clearly reveals God's presence is the brotherly charity of the faithful who are united in spirit as they work together for the faith of the Gospel, and who prove themselves a sign of unity." [20] In connection with this appeal for the unity of all believers the Council is also convinced of the necessity for co-operation and for a dialogue with unbelievers: "The Church sincerely proclaims that all men, believers and unbelievers alike, ought to work for the rightful betterment of this world in which all alike live. Such an ideal, however, cannot be realized without a sincere and prudent dialogue." [21]

It is irrelevant whether, in our dialogue with others, we use the term "natural law" or "natural moral law," or any other term. Genuine dialogue makes use of all possible starting points. One of these is an increasing awareness of the unity of all mankind, the hope of an ideal of future development which shall be more worthy of men, and the willingness to satisfy the general longing for peace and brotherhood.

If Christianity applies itself determinedly to the real problem of our time, in loyal co-operation with all men, if it works for a better future in a spirit of brotherliness and with respect for all men, then many who have hitherto refused to believe may find the hidden presence of God in this service and this hope.

Chapter 5

Love Must Be Open-Hearted

Literature and the arts are of great importance to the life of the Church   *no. 62*

Is the Sermon on the Mount [22] merely a collection of pious counsels, without binding force? Or is it a series of casuistical solutions to real problems, or of legal directives which claim validity for all times and in all places? The answer to these questions, and others similar to them, is of basic importance for the understanding of Christian ethics.

THE SERMON ON THE MOUNT: A NEW COVENANT

Through his chosen literary form and in the whole construction of the Sermon, Matthew makes it clear that he intends to contrast the New Law with the Covenant of the Old Testament.

Luke introduces his shorter version of the Sermon on the Mount with these words: "And he came down with them, and stood on a level place, with a great crowd of his disciples, and a great multitude of people" (Lk 6:17). Jesus reveals the power of God's kingdom which has been made manifest in him: "All the crowd sought to touch him." In Matthew's more literary version the presence of the multitude of people, and the close bond of friendship between Jesus and his chosen disciples, are also clearly emphasized. "Seeing the crowds, he went up on the mountain,

57

5

and when he sat down his disciples came to him. And he opened his mouth and taught them" (Mt 5:1-2). In both Gospels the closeness of the Lord to his own followers and his attitude to the multitude of people, his mission as Savior and his full authority to proclaim the Law are emphasized for all to see. The presence of Emmanuel is still more eloquently described by Luke in his account of the descent from the mountain on which Jesus had called his apostles to him by name (Lk 6:12-16). Why does Matthew say that Jesus climbed the mountain in order to proclaim his Beatitudes there? The answer is to be found in Matthew's Jewish-Christian readers or listeners, and the analogy with the Covenant and the giving of the Tables of the Law on Sinai: "The Lord said to Moses, 'Cut two tables of stone like the first; and I will write upon the tables the words that were on the first tables, which you broke. Be ready in the morning, and come up in the morning to Mount Sinai, and present yourself there to me on the top of the mountain. No man shall come up with you, and let no man be seen throughout all the mountain; let no flocks or herds feed before that mountain'" (Ex 34:1-3; cf. Ex 19: 17-25).

The people of Israel, in their hardness of heart, were not in a fit state to approach the sacred mountain. God's revelation, it is true, was for the sake of granting them the Covenant, but it signified mercy for a terror-stricken and stiff-necked people. The Mount of the Beatitudes is very different: we see the closeness of Jesus to his disciples and to the multitudes of people. It was not only that the proclamation of the Beatitudes replaced the thunder and lightning of the Old Covenant. It was also a new way of presenting a new Covenant: this one came to us in the person of Emmanuel. It was not by pure chance that Matthew added the words, "And he sat down . . . opened his lips and taught them" (Mt 5:1-2). Here we have the solemn expression of the teacher's authority.

The nine Beatitudes express perfection, the full attainment of salvation. Luke deliberately chooses four of these, in order to remind his Hellenic followers of the number of the cardinal virtues. He sternly emphasizes the binding character of the Beatitudes by adding to each one the cry of "Woe!" to those who reject them. In Matthew, immediately after the nine Beatitudes the distinctive character of discipleship is expressed in the image of the "salt of the earth." "You are the salt of the earth, but if salt has lost its taste, how shall its saltness be restored? It is no longer good for anything, except to be thrown out and trodden underfoot by men" (Mt 5:13).

The fact that we have here an authoritative proclamation of the new Covenant is made still more clear in the words: "Think not that I have come to abolish the law and the prophets; I have come not to abolish them but to fulfill them" (Mt 5:17). Jesus is therefore not merely a scribe, not merely a commentator on the law of Sinai and the prophets. He is the One in whom all things shall be fulfilled.

Matthew then deliberately repeats the contrasting antitheses: "You have heard that it was said by the men of old . . . but I say to you . . . ." We shall have to return once more to the substance of these contrasting codes when we wish to demonstrate the originality of the new Covenant. But the literary form itself is a clear indication of Matthew's intention to emphasize the significance of the Sermon on the Mount as the expression of the New Pact.

As we read the Sermon it becomes increasingly clear that, apart from its message of love, it makes demanding claims on men. Christ binds the people — the disciples in a more intimate way, but also the multitude around him — to his own person, in order to persuade them to do the will of his Father. "Not everyone who says to me, 'Lord, Lord' shall enter the kingdom of Heaven, but he who does the will of my Father who is in Heaven." The absolute nature of this obligation is emphasized by the vision of the judgment which will separate his followers from those who reject his teaching: "On that day many will say to me, 'Lord, Lord'. . . . And then will I declare to them: 'I never knew you'" (Mt 7:21-23).

Salvation or damnation depends on the believer's acceptance of the Sermon on the Mount and obedience to its precepts. This is expressed at the conclusion of the Sermon by Matthew (7:24-27) and Luke (6:47-49) in almost identical words: "Everyone then who hears these words of mine and does them will be like a wise man . . . ." Whoever refuses to accept the Sermon on the Mount as a directive for life is comparable to the fool who built his house upon sand.

The Evangelist's concluding words once more stress the binding character of the Sermon on the Mount. "And when Jesus had finished these sayings, the crowds were astonished at his teaching, for he taught them as one who had authority, and not as their scribes" (Mt 7:28-29).

In both religious and civic education, special care must be given to the proper formation of youth.   no. 89

The wonderful harmony between the supreme authority of Jesus and his closeness to his disciples and to the multitudes of people is expressed in a unique way by Matthew in his literary version of the Sermon on the Mount. By way of analogy one can refer to the Johannine synthesis of Jesus' moral doctrine. On another occasion Jesus, the bearer of salvation, of the Good News and the New Law, appears in a supreme and incomparably close intimacy with his disciples, in a revelation of infinite love and at the same time of absolute authority. Jesus the host washes the feet of his apostles, saying: "You call me Teacher and Lord, and you are right, for so I am" (Jn 13:13).

THE BEATITUDES: DOCTRINE AND GOOD NEWS

What is presumably the oldest extant summary of Jesus' initial preaching of the Gospel (Mk 1:14-15) already shows the essential unity between the offer of salvation and the conditions for attaining it. The good news that the "fullness of time" has come and that the kingdom of heaven is near contains the call to salvation which in itself heralds the long awaited Messianic peace. "The time is fulfilled and the kingdom of God is at

60

hand; repent and believe in the Gospel." The demand for a totally new dispensation and for a total conversion to God finds its foundation and its transforming power in the Gospel, which is the message of salvation. The transformation is effected in faith, in grateful acceptance of the glad tidings, and in conversion. This basic relationship between the joyful reality of salvation and a new redeemed life is wonderfully described in John's account of the Sermon on the Mount and of the farewell words of Jesus. Already in the Old Testament the Covenant is seen as wholly dependent upon God's mercy. But the face of Israel's hard-heartedness the "thou shalt" is as formidable as a solitary high peak, or as thunder and lightning. The new Covenant, in its solemnity and binding force, is by no means inferior to the old Pact. But its quality of mercy and its firm foundation in faith in the Good News are incomparably more evident. The Beatitudes contain doctrine, and this doctrine is in itself a Beatitude; it is good news and the joyful reality of salvation.

The proclamation of God's gift and command contains also an imperative obligation, but expressed in such a way that the "imperative" never acquires the harshness of the earlier Pact. "You are the salt of the earth" (Mt 5:13) is part of a gracious appeal. But the proclamation of salvation confronts man with a decision: "You are the light of the world." The fact of salvation which Christ, who is the true light, illuminates for us so brightly in order that we also give light to the world, inevitably includes the command: "Let your light so shine . . ." (Mt 5:14-16). The same basic imperative is also to be found in a synthesis of John's Gospel. The announcement of the New Law is preceded by that of the new life, not only to be won through the example and by the authority of Jesus but also explicitly and emphatically indicated as our new existence in Christ by virtue of the power of the Holy Spirit. The commandment "Love one another as I have loved you" (Jn 15:12) is wholly based on the teaching of salvation expressed in the words: "I am the true vine and my father is the vine-dresser" and ". . . now you are already made clean by the word which I have spoken to you." And the command to seek salvation is heard again in the appeal "Abide in me" (Jn 15:1-4).

The sublimity of the command corresponds to the sublimity of the gift and of the vocation. The unity of the whole message, the total fusion of the obligation with the offer of salvation, is an essential aspect of the mandatory character of the Sermon on the Mount.

LOVE: THE ESSENTIAL CONTENT OF THE LAW

The climax of the proclamation: "But I say to you," is at the same time also the synopsis or synthesis of the doctrine contained in the new Covenant: "Love your enemies and pray for those who persecute you, so that you may be sons of your Father who is in Heaven; for he makes his sun rise on the evil and on the good, and sends rain on the just and the unjust" and "You therefore must be perfect as your heavenly Father is perfect" (Mt 5:43-48). In the total context, the mercy which God showed us in sending us his Son and giving us the Covenant of salvation is pre-eminent. In this light, however, God's forbearance, kindness and mercy, shown in his creation and his providence, also become clearly visible.

Through the new Covenant and God's spiritual nearness to his people, we learn of our capacity, and therefore also of our obligation, to imitate God above all in this quality of mercy. The command to seek perfection must not in this connection be confused with an ethical code of anthropocentric self-improvement, or with an abstract ideal of moral perfection. It is a question of the gradual assimilation of the people, who are entirely dependent on the grace and mercy of God, with their Lord. In his shorter version of the Sermon on the Mount, Luke also has in mind this imitation of the Lord when he quotes the command: "Love your enemies," but in this connection he completes the demand for perfection with the exhortation: "Be merciful, even as your Father is merciful" (Lk 6:35-36).

Whereas in Luke and Matthew the central commandment bears a reference to the heavenly Father, John's formulation of the new and all-embracing Covenant also emphasizes the Christocentric concept: "This is my commandment, that you love one another as I have loved you" (Jn 15:12). The two attitudes complement each other. It is emphasized in John's Gospel that Christ directs our gaze towards the Father: "He who has seen me has seen the Father" and "The words that I say to you I do not speak on my own authority; but the Father who dwells in me does his works" (Jn 14:10).

One must not overlook the difference between the account given by John and that given by Matthew. John quite explicitly presents the moral-religious doctrine in the context of the Easter mystery, in the Eucharist, in the coming of the Holy Spirit and in our mystical share in the supernatural love of the Father and the Son. Love for one's neighbor is,

The horror and perversity of war are immensely magnified by the multiplication of scientific weapons.   no. 80

according to the new Covenant, a proof of life in Christ and of the "indwelling" of his word in a disciple. But in Matthew too it is the gracious gift of discipleship and the wonderful power of Jesus' words which produce the sublime and unprecedented command of love, and in fact so much so that this command does not appear, or at least does not primarily appear, as a demand from without, but rather as the result within the soul of the all-compelling power of the Gospel and of the new discipleship.[23] In this connection it is taken for granted by both Evangelists that the disciple is not oppressed or overwhelmed by this power, but is by it released into true freedom. If he does not trust himself entirely to Christ's word then he remains in the old bondage.

OLD PROHIBITION, NEW GOAL

In its literary form the Sermon on the Mount itself makes it evident that here it was a question of a completely new kind of law, different from the Old Law which still dominated the school of the Scribes: "You have heard that it was said: 'You shall not commit adultery.' But I say to you that every one who looks at a woman lustfully, has already committed adultery with her in his heart" (Mt 5:27-28).

The prohibitions of the Old Law are not challenged. Nor is there even the slightest trace of a tendency towards that doctrine of "situation ethics" which, with the excuse of the universal imperative of love, draws the conclusion that everything, even adultery and perjury, can be justified in a context of true charity. But the mere observance of these fixed standards is shown to be absolutely inadequate under the new justification. "Unless your righteousness exceeds that of the scribes and Pharisees you will never enter the kingdom of Heaven" (Mt 5:20). These words form the introduction to the emphatic repetition: "It was said to men of old . . . but I say to you . . . ."

Even if the negative aspect of the law, seen in the traditional teaching of the Decalogue, is not challenged, nevertheless much more than the mere addition of a few more commandments is required. It is more a case of adjusting one's emphasis, changing one's whole attitude: the disciple of Christ is no longer confronted with a series of prohibitions. He needs them only because he has not yet found sufficient strength to turn

65

his attention elsewhere. The seven repetitions of "But I say to you . . ." stress that the new Gospel is orientated towards a different goal.

A man who has accepted the new Covenant expressed in the Beatitudes has not the least desire to disobey the prohibitions: Thou shalt not kill! Thou shalt not commit adultery! Nor will he pride himself on not having transgressed these low-pitched commandments. He will not boast: "I have done all this from my youth," for he knows that he cannot enter the kingdom of God which is already here with us unless he seeks to obey the demand for perfection "as your Father in Heaven is perfect." The transition to this new attitude is absolutely necessary.

The New Testament proclamation of the moral law and the obligations of discipleship are founded on a response to the general call to holiness. The chief object of Christian morality is the "sublime vocation of all who believe in Christ." [24]

The Sermon on the Mount makes it absolutely clear that the fundamental law for Christ's disciples lies in the directives for life indicated in the Beatitudes, the "glad tidings" of grace and of the kingdom of God, which is coming in all its power. These directives which are all comprised in the one command: "Be perfect therefore, as your Father in Heaven is perfect" are no less solemn than the binding commandments of the Decalogue and are equally imperative. But the word "law" here takes on a new meaning and becomes a dynamic movement, a pilgrimage.

Matthew, in the parable of the talents (25: 14-30), gives an important clue to the understanding of this dynamic law which directs us to the goal. The man who fully utilizes his two talents receives the same praise as the man who has made a profit out of his five. Paul explains still more succinctly the uniqueness of the "law of the Spirit" (Rm 8:2) or the law of faith (Rm 3:31).

In all things it is a question of a grateful assent which opens the door to true freedom, to the grace of God in Christ Jesus: "Grace was given to each of us according to the measure of Christ's gift" (Ep 4:7). The "I say to you" of the Sermon on the Mount is a dynamic law which can only be obeyed in a continual "straining forward," a constant striving, such as St. Paul described: "Not that I have already obtained this or am already perfect; but I press on to make it my own, because Christ Jesus has made me his own. Brethren, I do not consider that I have made it my own; but one thing I do, forgetting what lies behind and straining forward to what lies ahead. I press on toward the goal for the prize of the upward call of God in Jesus Christ. Let those of us who are mature be thus minded . . ." (Ph 3:13-15).

THE DISCERNING OF SPIRITS

In chapter 3 of St. Matthew's Gospel the shifting of emphasis from prohibitions to directives is clearly evident, and even the meaning of the word "commandment" is no longer understood in the same way. In chapter 6, and to some extent in chapter 7 also, more stress is laid on genuine piety and a genuine change of heart. These criteria concern the true nature of our love of God and for our fellow men. Here it should be noted that already at the end of chapter 5, which leads directly to the presentation of the new goal set before us, the love of our enemies is set before us as the pre-eminent sign of newness of life. Then we are told also to cultivate the pure intention of honoring God (6:1), and to show love to our fellow men for no ulterior motive (6:2-4). Ostentatious prayer is no sign of newness of life (6:5-6). At this point comes the command to pray in the right manner, but the willingness to forgive others

is especially stressed as a proof of humility before God. To illustrate the totally new meaning of the first Beatitude, there follows a description of the characteristics of the spirit of poverty and of trust in God (6:19-34).

In accordance with the first Beatitude, which exalts this spirit of poverty and humility, kind understanding and abstention from harsh judgments are presented as proofs of conversion to the new Law (7:1-5). Chapter 7, verse 6 stresses the need for discretion in dialogue with others. We must see that the Word, and above all the message of salvation, are offered at the right time and according to the recipient's readiness to listen. Love also controls the proclamation of the truth. A proper attitude of faith, and of love for God are shown in the habit of trustful prayer (7:7-11).

Matthew (7:12) gives us as the final criterion the Golden Rule. But here it is undoubtedly offered as a positive commandment, whereas in Tobit 4:15 it is found in a negative formula: "What you hate, do not do to anyone." The addition of the words "for this is the law and the prophets" indicates continuity of doctrine and acknowledges the validity of the old proverbial wisdom in the

Agencies of the international community should do their part to provide for the various necessities of men in the areas of food, health, education and employment.   no. 84

"discerning of spirits." The final criterion, which already leads to the general conclusion in which the binding force of Christ's words is emphasized, is characteristically generic and comprehensive: "You will know them by their fruits" (7:20). Our hearts eagerly accept the ethics of the Sermon on the Mount, inspired by the power of the message of salvation, but at the same time the Sermon makes it clear that the change of heart through faith in God must transform our whole life. These words can be understood in this sense: "Either make the tree good and its fruits good, or make the tree bad, and its fruits bad" (Mt 12:33).

FREEDOM UNDER BINDING LAW

There can be no doubt that Matthew sees in the Sermon on the Mount the presentation of the Law which binds absolutely but also leads to freedom. It is also clear from the whole context that he has not the slightest intention of blurring the outlines of the Ten Commandments, which contain so many prohibitions. The new directives are not intended to be counsels of perfection which have not necessarily any binding force. Everyone must adopt the spirit here described and set out determinedly on his way in the direction so clearly indicated.

But the directives, or at least many of them, are formulated in such a way that they cannot be used as "casuistical solutions" for all possible cases. A completely literal interpretation, such as is still found in current handbooks on morals, would have to understand from Matthew 5:33-37 that the Christian must not, under any circumstances take an oath. He must say "Yes" when he means "Yes," and "No" when he means "No": "Anything more than these comes from evil." The text states quite unambiguously that the Christian must strive after absolute simplicity and sincerity in his speech, and in fact do this so diligently that a simple "Yes" will suffice to inspire confidence. Yet ecclesiastical tradition and legislation have not felt bound, by means of strictly formulated declarations, to forbid oaths in all circumstances. It may in exceptional cases be necessary for a Christian to swear an oath. But if Christians themselves, through habitual insincerity, make this necessary, then it obviously "comes from evil."

Matthew 5:38-42 provides the basic doctrine of the correct response to force, namely, the power of a strong and selfless love which finally overcomes all evil. This is a binding principle. But the offering of the other cheek after the first blow, or the payment of damages to the plaintiff when any legal contest over property occurs, and other similar procedures, are not to be imitated literally in all circumstances. Diversely it might even seem from Matthew's Gospel (5:42) that we are implicitly bound to lend to everyone indiscriminately on request (5:42).

The violent images of plucking out the right eye and cutting off the right hand (5:29-30) teach us the serious effort which the Christian must make to free himself from all that prevents him from total acceptance of God's authority. But this by no means solves the question, often a very complex one, of the avoidance of a necessary or unnecessary occasion of sin. This must nevertheless be considered in the spirit of Christian resolution. On the other hand, these words in the Gospel certainly do not justify a rigoristic interpretation of the Sermon which indiscriminatingly demands from all what is psychologically impossible for many.

Judging within this context the words "Whoever marries a divorced woman commits adultery" are not in themselves alone a sufficient proof that under the new Law the second marriage of an innocent party in a divorce excludes that person from God's kingdom, whatever the circumstances. The Pauline privilege, which is in pastoral practice widely extended, would contradict the notion that in these words of the Sermon on the Mount there is an absolute and irreversible legal sanction. In contrast to the facility and light-heartedness with which, according to the teaching of the Pharisees, a man could divorce his wife, the Sermon on the Mount stresses the absolute need for fidelity as a norm of marriage even when this implies grave sacrifices. From the biblical text alone, especially considered in its context, we are unable to decide whether the practice of many Orthodox churches, which from time immemorial have admitted to the sacraments the innocent partner in a divorce on the occasion of a new marriage, does or does not violate the true concept of marriage. One must also study all the pronouncements of the Bible, of tradition and of the Church. If everything possible is done to strengthen the intention of absolute fidelity, even at the cost of courageous self-denial, then the Church may permit herself great tolerance, in the spirit of the Sermon on the Mount, towards people in hopeless situations, as long as they really show good will.

With regard to the reform of ecclesiastical law, now in progress, one may well ask the question whether Canon 1130: "The innocent spouse . . . is never bound by any obligation of restoring the adulterous spouse to the conjugal relationship" still satisfactorily agrees with the teaching of the Sermon on the Mount, especially in view of the fact that in the modern world divorce leads in most cases to a second marriage of the other partner. Naturally we must clearly distinguish between a legal position and a binding moral principle. Presumably the Canon means only that no juridical obligation and no legal sanction can force the "innocent spouse" to resume marital life with the adulterous partner. Since, however, it is a case of a "holy law" and for pastoral considerations great care is needed to avoid any misunderstandings, then in Canon Law the best possible solution for every specific case should be adopted, so that no one may fail to aspire to the goal set before us in the Sermon on the Mount: our union with the mercifully redeeming love of God. It may be possible to reconcile these two attitudes if, on the one hand, no juridical sanctions or legal obligations are imposed, while on the other hand the religious-moral law is clearly stated. Then the innocent spouse will humbly ask himself in what way he has failed, and, according to his situation, he will do all he can to save his partner by renewed fidelity and love.

The Sermon on the Mount cannot be treated lightly, as if everything it contained were a mere counsel of perfection. On the other hand, there is no legal harshness about it. It teaches us what our generous answer to God's love should be, and makes its appeal to the mature Christian who grows in the knowledge of Christ and therefore also in determination to reach his goal so that, in the knowledge of the true nature of love, he may here and now set out on the road to love's fulfillment.

In the preceding chapter we arrived at the conclusion that in many respects the Sermon on the Mount certainly contains principles binding for all Christians. But, in connection with this, modern man is faced with the question: How can the binding character of an ethical code which was revealed once for all be reconciled with the multiplicity of cultures and the historical development of man? Erich Fromm speaks for many of our contemporaries when he asserts that moral principles are based on the knowledge of man's nature and not on revelation or on man-made laws or agreements.[25] When divine revelation imposes permanent principles at any definite historical moment, would this not be like the behavior of parents who would fit their children out at a given moment in their childhood with clothes they are to wear for the rest of their lives?

In my opinion we do not need atheists to help us to preach true love, as long as the prophetic spirit and courage still flourish in the Church. But even the hope we place in this prophetic spirit does not exempt us from the obligation of a serious discussion of the question put forward by Erich Fromm and many other enquiring minds: Does the assertion that moral principles are divinely revealed not in itself lead to an

While rejecting atheism, root and branch, the Church sincerely professes that all men, believers and unbelievers alike, ought to work for a rightful betterment of this world in which all alike live.   no. 21

estrangement from life, and to the immobility of a morality founded on religious sanctions? Are those who challenge the immutability of a moral code founded on religion not already convinced that they cannot be true prophets and remain within the Church?

It is quite clear that in this connection we must distinguish very sharply between the situation of Israel and that of the Christian Church. In the case of many religious-moral principles of the Old Testament it was very largely a matter of keeping Israel uncontaminated from seductive heathen cults and civilizations. The Jewish ethical code had a fundamental religious significance but it also contained the very great danger of imprisoning Israel in a traditionalistic national world of its own. Christianity, instead, is a missionary religion, intended for all people of all cultures. The transition from the protective religion of Israel to the universal missionary religion of Christ did not however take place without the greatest difficulty. Perhaps we must admit that it is not yet fully completed, in spite of all the determined efforts of the Apostle of the Gentiles.

REVEALED AND LEGAL ETHICS

Rudolf Otto, the religious historian and theologian, has, by his distinction between sacred and legalized moral laws, made a considerable contribution to our theme.[26] By the term sacred moral laws he means the moral response to the numinous element in the Christian's outlook, to the divinely revealed holiness and goodness of God. In religious experience the believing, hoping, trusting and adoring attitude to God takes precedence over man's duties to his fellows. But, since the attitude of faith and worship has an integrating power, it increasingly claims man's whole life. Whatever he recognizes to be right and proper he now also acknowledges as something due to God, something which contains in itself a religious sanction. The response to God is in this way given life and positive content. Rudolf Otto calls it the "schematization" of our experience of the numinous. The expression is somewhat debatable but the way in which Otto explains it is very much to the point: the more perfect the religious experience, the more nearly do the sacred *ethos* and the sanctioned *ethos* approach a genuine synthesis. It is only by the imperfection of religious experience that the

73

inconsistency or stark irreconcilability of religion and morality, and a purely formalistic schematization, can be explained.

How far does the principle laid down by Rudolf Otto apply to Old Testament religion and morality?

Abraham inherited, from his own cultural environment, certain moral concepts such as the obligations of hospitality and the responsibilities of kinship. A moderate form of polygamy was not considered blameworthy. Abraham believed in God and trusted himself wholly to God's guidance. His moral concepts contained religious sanctions derived from his religious faith, and these were not completely transformed. With a good conscience he took to himself Agar as well as Sarah for a wife when Sarah was seen to be barren. He seems to have divorced Agar with an equally good conscience, without any juridical formalities, because his action was accepted as right in his own patriarchal society.

By virtue of the Covenant established with Moses, the whole tribe of Israel came under the Law. Their obligations towards the tribe as a whole and towards each individual member were strengthened by religious sanctions. It was not a divine revelation but a complex of

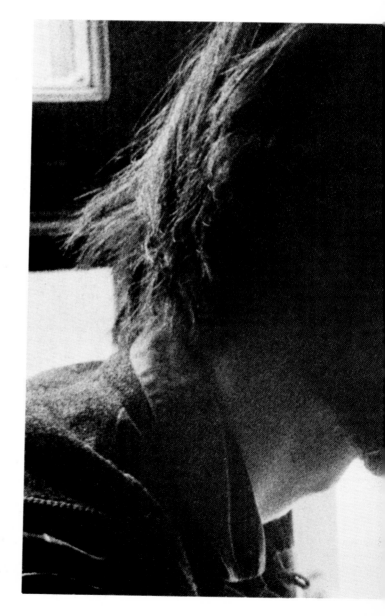

... is rooted in the conjugal covenant of irrevocable personal consent.   *no. 48*

traditions and of economic and social conditions which made polygamy acceptable within certain limits, and also made the marriage of Levites compulsory. Divorce was not allowed by divine revelation but existed as a loose arrangement under the Law. It then gradually fell into disrepute and its rules were tightened. The sacred principles of the Covenant, together with consequent cultural transformations, gradually led to the prevalence of monogamy, but not to the total abolition of divorce, which was still maintained within legal bounds. The position of women remained largely that found in all patriarchal civilizations, and changed with the total structural changes of social, economic and cultural life. Of course we must not overlook the effect of religion on the continual development of the moral code. In the long run religion must exert its influence on all social relationships when it is generally believed that not only man but woman also is created in the image and likeness of God.

Revelation is above all a religious experience, but it also throws light on the relations between persons and above all on the person's relationship to the community in which he lives. Religion reveals the great truth: it is impossible to love God without loving our neighbor. But the all-embracing commandment of loving our fellow men derived its meaning from the realities of every day life, from the solidarity of the tribe: the hostile Egyptian or Canaanite is not accepted as a neighbor. Only gradually does belief in one God and Creator enlarge the horizon so that the "stranger" will be accepted as a "neighbor."

In the light of modern biblical exegesis, we can presumably argue that we are by no means bound to believe that the individual moral principles of the Old Testament were derived from direct revelation. When we come to define the content of the moral law we find that most rules originate in tradition, in man's knowledge as conditioned by his environment. But the general outlook, the synthesis, owes more and more to faith, to our experience of God and to revelation. Faith is an enzyme, a leaven which gradually also refines, purifies and inspires moral standards, with solicitude for our neighbor's needs and for those of the whole community in the sight of God.

Since Israel was a nation governed by a paternalistic regime, which needed a great number of detailed rules and, above all, since monotheism was protected by a great number of religious statutes, there resulted for the people an increasingly meaningless routine, conventional and formalistic. It is the great merit of the prophets that they did all they could to oppose this. It is here above all that the influence of revelation can be seen. The prophets, inspired by their faith, were sent to restore true moral values. In this sense revelation means precisely the opposite of schematization or conventionalism.

When God's spirit descends on a man it profoundly alters him. Their experience of the living God led the prophets to try to persuade the people to consider attentively the realities of this life and the needs of the whole community.

GOD'S COMMAND: A DYNAMIC INVITATION

The revelation vouchsafed to Israel is fundamentally different from any abstract philosophy. It is God's manifestation of himself in our life; it consists of God's intervention in history, and the claim he makes on us here and now, indeed in such a way that a relationship of trust is built up. In saying this of course we neither exclude nor deny that generally valid moral principles are to be found in Holy Scripture, in the Old and above all in the New Testament. But we have chiefly to do with positive instructions to a particular nation in an actual historical situation, and from these we may also discern some permanent directives for all future generations.

Therefore we probably do not need, for example, to believe that Abraham received the order to offer Isaac as a sacrifice through a specific intervention. Although he certainly believed in God's promises he still felt bound in his conscience to sacrifice his son Isaac, in accordance with the traditional concepts he had inherited.[27] His outlook, although that of a believer, was substantially influenced by the traditions of his race. His environmental culture took for granted that in certain circumstances God required a human sacrifice, even that of a firstborn son. Abraham was pleasing to God because of his willingness to serve him to the best of his knowledge. But at this point he experienced a divine revelation which taught him that the God of mercy did not demand any human sacrifice. Here we have a positive command and a divine intervention which are to determine future moral concepts also. From that day on the firstborn son was to be spared. Only the first litter of animals was still to be sacrificed. The heroic readiness to sacrifice even one's best beloved to the Lord, and the dawn of new knowledge, are preserved in the story of Isaac's intended sacrifice and in the ransom of the firstborn child.

*Technology is now transforming the face of the earth and trying to
master outer space.   no. 5*

God truly spoke to his people through the prophets. The experience of the justice and compassion of God, which was expounded by the great religious leaders and prophets who were taught by God, threw new light on many vital questions.

Christ brought us something more than the message of the love and compassion of our heavenly Father. He not only represented in his own person, and announced, a sacred ethos. He is also the perfect revelation and incarnation of the all-embracing love of our fellows. The early Christian community, and the Evangelist who gave a final literary form to the Sermon on the Mount, understood him aright. He not only imparted a spirit of faith, and a belief in his own crucifixion and resurrection, but also left us instructions for a new life to be lived by faith in him. His commandments point the way for all time. The question is however: In what direction? By their literal application without reference to changing times and cultures, or by their acceptance as the final foundation of faith and a final orientation for life? Hardly.

Christ is the ultimate Word of the Father to mankind; he is true God and perfect man. But he did not assume his human nature in an environment and culture common to all men, but in the particular environment and culture of Israel. In the every day life of Nazareth he responded to the very real problems of his fellow men. When he answered their questions he did not express merely an abstract proverbial wisdom but spoke in parables, constantly making use of personal experiences common in the lives of his listeners. In his kingdom he has room for all, even for the humblest sinners, for all who are spiritually awakened, if they will only come to him in all sincerity and believe in him.

If we are right in our belief that the Sermon on the Mount contains directives for the orientation of our whole lives, then many other New Testament laws could be interpreted in the same sense. On the one hand it is clear that Jesus himself and his apostles emphatically condemned certain modes of conduct as being in absolute contradiction to the spirit of true love and the sincere acceptance of the kingdom of God. On the other hand, the Lord felt much loving compassion for our poor human powers of perception which are conditioned by particular epochs and circumstances, and by a feeling of responsibility for the present order which is not yet replaceable. Christ knew men as they really were. The direction in which they should move is indicated, and the "discerning of spirits" is facilitated and encouraged. But plenty of room is left for multiplicity.

From the beginning, however, there existed difficulties concerning the general applicability of particular commands. Even the apostles did not see clearly, down to the smallest detail, the way in which Christianity was to respond to the universal nature of Christian vocation, in a great variety of cultures. Peter's conscience was perturbed when it was revealed to him that Jewish concepts of purity (meaning pure and impure food), of circumcision and of many other things could not be justified by reference to the Gospel. "But I said, 'No, Lord; for nothing common or unclean has ever entered my mouth'" (Ac 11:8). James himself had presumably not yet succeeded in making a final distinction between the absolute and the temporal, when he proposed his formula for compromise with the Gentile Christians: "Therefore my judgment is that we should not trouble those of the Gentiles who turn to God, but should write to them to abstain from the pollutions of idols and from unchastity and from what is strangled and from blood" (Ac 15:19-20).

This lingering perplexity and inability to distinguish between that which endures for ever and that which is conditioned by time will always re-emerge in the Church. Did Paul himself perhaps, the great pioneer of

missionary adaptability, see clearly how great an element of that which is conditioned by time is present in his arguments concerning the subordinate role of women, the status of the slave, and the place of woman in church assemblies? It was not for him to work out distinctions which were not yet mature, or necessary for his actual mission. But, following in his Master's footsteps, he already showed the spirit in which new questions would have to be solved.

Paul had certainly heard what the Lord had said about marriage and divorce. In all his preaching of the faith he advocated fidelity, forbearance and selfless love. But he did not offer a legal solution of the problems of those converts for whom married life with an unbelieving partner had become intolerable. He allowed divorce and re-marriage only when this was the only viable solution. But to the women who, in opposition to all moral law and to the spirit and letter of the Sermon on the Mount, had divorced their husbands, he says clearly and definitely that they should either return to their husbands or live as celibates (1 Cor 7:11).

In conclusion we may well say that a morality which is rooted in revelation should not be allowed to become overly formalized. Erich Fromm's demand that moral laws should be founded on human knowledge and experience, and not on a hard and fast rule based on revelation, must be taken into serious consideration, but without in any way diminishing the value of revealed truth and its claim on man. The divine revelation in Jesus Christ is the greatest possible contribution towards our knowledge of God and knowledge of man. It also presents a most imperative command to keep ourselves always receptive to new knowledge, for God still continues to work in history. Evolution is God's work, and therefore demands that man, within the limits prescribed for him, shall seek to obtain the truest possible knowledge of himself, of his fellow men and of the world in which we live. The final directive is given us here clearly and imperatively, in the name of God's love for us as revealed in Jesus Christ: we are told that we should try to show an ever more perfect obedience to the commandment to love, to the fullest extent of our powers. This doctrine does not immobilize us but gives us the strongest incentive to go forward, and protects us from the most dangerous interpretations.

Erich Fromm, and many other people who suffer under the same difficulties, can however accept our answer seriously only when we admit that we have too often in days gone by, had recourse to easy solutions to the new and urgent problems which arise from new cultural environments. The important thing for us here and now is that we be able to answer them in the affirmative when they ask: Have you learned something from the past?

Christians cannot yearn for anything more ardent.

han to serve the men of the modern world. no. 93

Notes

1. See the monumental work, of great historical value, by G. Barauna, V. Schurr (Hgg.), *Die Kirche in der Welt von heute,* a commentary on the Pastoral Constitution *Gaudium et Spes,* Salzburg, 1967.
2. *Gaudium et Spes,* No. 44.
3. *Op. cit.,* No. 20.
4. *Loc. cit.*
5. *Op. cit.,* No. 19.
6. *Op. cit.,* No. 2.
7. *Op. cit.,* No. 24.
8. Denzinger-Schönmetzer, No. 1799.
9. This chapter first appeared in: J. Ratzinger and J. Neumann (Hgg.), *Theologie im Wandel,* Facultät Tübingen, Freiburg-Munich, 1967, 211-227.
10. *Gaudium et Spes,* No. 43.
11. *Loc. cit.*
12. *Op. cit.,* No. 19.
13. *Loc. cit.*
14. *Op. cit.,* No. 21.
15. *Op. cit.,* No. 19.
16. *Op. cit.,* No. 51.
17. *Op. cit.,* No. 24.
18. *Op. cit.,* No. 21.
19. *Op. cit.,* No. 24.
20. *Op. cit.,* No. 21.
21. *Loc. cit.*
22. Cf. B. Lanwer, *Die Grundgedanken der Bergpredict auf dem Hintergrund des Alten Testaments und des Spätjudentums,* Hiltrup, 1934; H. Windisch, *Der Sinn der Bergpredigt,* Leipzig, 1937; H. Asmussen, *Die Bergpredigt,* Gottingen, 1939; Th. Soiron, *Die Bergpredigt Jesu,* Freiburg, 1944; M. Dibelius, *Die Bergpredigt,* in *Botschaft und Geschichte,* I, Tübingen, 1953, 79-174; J. Dupont, *Les Béatitudes,* Lowen, 1958; R. Schnackenburg, *Die sittliche Botschaft des Neuen Testamentes,* Munich, 1962, 30-55; J. Jeremias, *Die Bergpredigt,* Stuttgart, 1963; W. D. Davies, *The Setting of the Sermon on the Mount,* Cambridge, 1964; H. Thielicke, *Das Leben kann noch einmal beginnen, Ein Gang durch die Bergpredigt,* Stuttgart, 1965.
23. This is the thesis of J. Jeremias, *Die Bergpredigt,* Stuttgart, 1963, according to which the Sermon on the Mount could be used as a catechism for the newly baptized; it seems very plausible.
24. Decree *Optatam Totius,* No. 16.
25. E. Fromm, *The Heart of Man, Its Genius for Good and Evil,* New York, 1962, 13.
26. Cf. R. Otto, *Aufsätze das Numinose betreffend,* Stuttgart-Gotha, 1923, 179-186, also *Das Heilige,* Munich, 1936, 69 et seq. and 165 et seq.
27. Cf. W. Eichrodt, *Theologie des Alten Testaments,* I, Stuttgart-Gottingen, 1957, 88-91.

Photo Credits